T0362907

BORN IN 1952?
WHAT ELSE HAPPENED?

PUBLISHED BY BOOM BOOKS
www.boombooks.biz

ABOUT THIS SERIES

.... But after that, I realised that I knew very little about these parents of mine. They had been born about the start of the Twentieth Century, and they died in 1970 and 1980. For their last 50 years, I was old enough to speak with a bit of sense.

I could have talked to them a lot about their lives. I could have found out about the times they lived in. But I did not. I know almost nothing about them really. Their courtship? Working in the pits? The Lock-out in the Depression? Losing their second child? Being dusted as a miner? The shootings at Rothbury? My uncles killed in the War? Love on the dole? There were hundreds, thousands of questions that I would now like to ask them. But, alas, I can't. It's too late.

Thus, prompted by my guilt, I resolved to write these books. They describe happenings that affected people, real people. The whole series is, to coin a modern phrase, designed to push your buttons, to make you remember and wonder at things forgotten.

The books might just let nostalgia see the light of day, so that oldies and youngies will talk about the past and re-discover a heritage otherwise forgotten. Hopefully, they will spark discussions between generations, and foster the asking and answering of questions that should not remain unanswered.

BORN IN 1952?

WHAT ELSE HAPPENED?

RON WILLIAMS

AUSTRALIAN SOCIAL HISTORY

BOOK 14 IN A SERIES OF 34 FROM 1939 to 1972

War Babies Years (1939 to 1945):   7 Titles
Baby Boom Years (1946 to 1960):   15 Titles
Post Boom Years (1961 to 1972):   12 Titles

BOOM, BOOM BABY, BOOM

BORN IN 1952? WHAT ELSE HAPPENED?

Published by Boom Books
Wickham, NSW, Australia
Web: www.boombooks.biz
Email: email@boombooks.biz

© Ron Williams 2013. This edition 2021

Creator: Williams, Ron, 1934- author.

Title: Born in 1952? : what else happened?

ISBN: 9780994601520

Subjects:Australia--History--Miscellanea--20th century.

Cover image: National Archives of Australia

A1200 6812646 Fruit picking

C4078 1650405 Telephonists at work

A1200 6812600 Play centre

Wiki Commons: Lew Hoad, national service

TABLE OF CONTENTS

SOME IMPORTANT PEOPLE AND EVENTS

Prime Minister	Bob Menzies
King of Britain till Jan 5	George VI
Queen of Britain after Jan 5th	Elizabeth II
Governor General	William McKell
Leader of Opposition	Doc Evatt
Governor General	William McKell
US President	Harry Truman
PM of Britain	Winston Churchill
The Pope	Pius XII

Winner of Ashes:

1948	Australia 4 - 0
1951- 51	Australia 4 - 1
1953	England 1 - 0

Melbourne Cup Winners:

1951	Delta
1952	Dalray
1953	Wodalla

Academy Awards

Best Actor	Gary Cooper
Best Actress	Judy Holliday
Best Movie	Great' Show' Earth

PREFACE TO THE SERIES

This book is the 14th in a series of books that I have researched and written. It tells a story about a number of important or newsworthy Australia-centric events that happened in 1952. The series covers each of the years from 1939 to 1968, for a total of 30 books.

I developed my interest in writing these books a few years ago at a time when my children entered their teens. My own teens started in 1947, and I started trying to remember what had happened to me then. I thought of the big events first, like Saturday afternoon at the pictures, and cricket in the back yard, and the wonderful fun of going to Maitland on the train for school each day. Then I recalled some of the not-so-good things. I was an altar boy, and that meant three or four Masses a week. I might have thought I loved God at that stage, but I really hated his Masses. And the schoolboy bullies, like Greg Favell, and the hapless Freddie Bevan. Yet, to compensate for these, there was always the beautiful, black headed, blue-sailor-suited June Browne, who I was allowed to worship from a distance.

I also thought about my parents. Most of the major events that I lived through came to mind readily. But after that, I realised that I really knew very little about these parents of mine. They had been born about the start of the Twentieth Century, and they died in 1970 and 1980. For their last 20 years, I was old enough to speak with a bit of sense. I could have talked to them a lot about their lives. I could have found out about the times they lived in. But I did not. I know almost nothing about them really. Their courtship? Working in the pits? The Lock-out in the Depression?

Losing their second child? Being dusted as a miner? The shootings at Rothbury? My uncles killed in the War? There were hundreds, thousands of questions that I would now like to ask them. But, alas, I can't. It's too late.

Thus, prompted by my guilt, I resolved to write these books. They describe happenings that affected people, real people. In **1952,** there is some coverage of international affairs, but a lot more on social events within Australia. This book, and the whole series is, to coin a modern phrase, designed to push the reader's buttons, to make you remember and wonder at things forgotten. The books might just let nostalgia see the light of day, so that oldies and youngies will talk about the past and re-discover a heritage otherwise forgotten. Hopefully, they will spark discussions between generations, and foster the asking and the answering of questions that should not remain unanswered.

The sources of my material. I was born in 1934, so that I can remember well a great deal of what went on around me from 1939 onwards. But of course, the bulk of this book's material came from research. That meant that I spent many hours in front of a computer reading electronic versions of newspapers, magazines, Hansard, Ministers' Press releases and the like. My task was to sift out, **day-by-day**, those stories and events that would be of interest to the most readers. Then I supplemented these with materials from books, broadcasts, memoirs, biographies, government reports and statistics. And I talked to old-timers, one-on-one, and in organised groups, and to Baby Boomers about their recollections. People with stories to tell come out of the woodwork, and talk no end about the tragic and funny and commonplace events that have shaped their lives.

The presentation of each book. For each year, the end result is a collection of Chapters on many of the topics that concerned ordinary people in that year. I think I have covered most of the major issues that people then were interested in. On the other hand, in some cases I have dwelt a little on minor frivolous matters, perhaps to the detriment of more sober considerations. Still, in the long run, this makes the book more readable, and hopefully it will convey adequately the spirit of the times.

I have been **deliberately national in outlook**, so that readers elsewhere will feel comfortable that I am talking about matters that affected them personally. After all, housing shortages and strikes and juvenile delinquency involved **all** Australians, and other issues, such as problems overseas, had no State component in them. Overall, I expect I can make you wonder, remember, rage and giggle equally, no matter where you hail from.

BACKGROUND FROM 1951

The world had seen a lot of tough times since the start of WWII in 1939. Firstly, there were the dreadful seven years of the wars in Europe and the Asia-Pacific. This was a period marred by thoughts and reality of death, of long-term separation from loved ones, of austerity and rationing, and of repression of freedoms for the common good.

It was followed by a period, from mid-1945, for half a decade, when Australians slowly kicked the war habit. There was diminishing need for austerity, rationing could be relaxed, regulations and constraints could be lifted. The world was a better place, a safer place, but still there was the shadow of the dreadful War years haunting many lives. As well, there were the many kill-joys in high positions who had enjoyed the power that war had given them, and **who stood firmly in the way of returning to normal.** Thus, for example, butter rationing continued till 1949, and petrol rationing till 1950. **Price controls on rents**, and on most goods and services, on banking, on imports, on what-have-you, were still very evident. Still, there were fewer blackouts, no tank traps on the beaches, and it was all much, much better than war. Though, as a young lad, I did miss the searchlights at night.

The fun started about 1950. After Bob Menzies got his title of Prime Minister back, the Baby Boomers took over. This horde of revellers were now thinking about their second child, starting to build a house in the developing housing estates on the fringes of cities, and buying a car on hire purchase. Hills Hoist sales were booming, jobs were easy to get in most years, electric lawn-mowers could be afforded, and most people by now had a 40-hour week. So life was good and getting better. On top of that, the coming decade saw **the embarrassment of a few Tall Poppies,** like Dr Evatt in the Petrov Case, and Bob Menzies in the Suez Affair. What more could you ask?

So, here we are in 1952. The previous year had been marred by some serious events. The Korean War that started in 1950 was still dragging on. This was supposedly a Civil War between North and South Korea, but was really just a trial of strength between the Capitalist USA, on the one hand, and Communist China and Russia, on the other. The battle-lines had moved south, then moved north, up to the border with China. About that time, the US Commander, Douglas MacArthur, was keen to press on and take on the full might of the Chinese and Russian States. But that would have involved another world war. So, when he persisted, **he was sacked by President Truman, and sent home to America**. Meanwhile the fighting continued, and the battle-lines now settled around the 38th Parallel, near the middle of the Korean Peninsular. Negotiations between the interested parties, and with the UN, were always going on, but **no one was at all serious about these**, and there was **no hope** that peace might break out soon.

Korea Continues. At the moment, the actual fighting in Korea was at a minimum because it was winter there. That meant snow and blizzards for the ground forces, and poor visibility for the bombers. Still, both sides managed to kill hundreds of each other every week, so the futile tragedy went on. And on.

Negotiations that might lead to peace had started about nine months ago. But, as I mentioned earlier, there was not much prospect of anyone backing off. For example, one matter for discussion was the swapping of prisoners of war. At the moment, the Allies held 45,000 prisoners, and the North Koreans held 50,000, mainly from South Korea and America. The obvious thing to do, as had been done in WWII, was to say these bodies of men were about equal, and swap the one for the other. But, no! There was no propaganda value in that.

The Americans wanted to somehow balance the books by allowing 5,000 North Korean citizens to cross over to the South, to "escape the tyranny of living under Communism."

After that, as an alternative, they proposed interviewing all 45,000 prisoners that they held, to make sure that **every single one of them wanted to be repatriated to their own country**. On the other side, the North Koreans were making equally silly and time-consuming proposals that guaranteed that no progress towards peace was made at all, and that the men in the trenches were buried there.

Other tragic news marred the 1951 year. **Ben Chifley died suddenly**. He was, and still is, much respected as a Prime Minister, and the nation was much saddened by his death. A young woman, Jean Lee, was convicted in Victoria of murder, and was executed. She was the last female to be executed in Australia.

Politically, Prime Minster Bob Menzies tried to scare the nation with his **never-ending campaign against Communism**, and had tried to outlaw that Party. In 1951 he held a national referendum on the matter, but it failed. At the same time, all young men of 18 years of age were conscripted into National Service, for 14 weeks in the first year, and for follow-up periods over the next three years. This was all part of the **Red menace theme that Menzies continued to push**.

But we had some lighter happenings as well. Massive celebrations were held in January to mark the 50th anniversary of the forming of the Australian Federation. In the suburbs, Sundays were full of fun as the afternoon nap was destroyed by the sounds of electric mowers by the dozen. In the city centres, a few brave entrepreneurs opened movie theatres for public viewing of movies, but such waywardness was being highly criticised.

In all, life was good for most people. Mortgages could be got if you crawled hard enough to a bank manager. People were getting a decent wage, working conditions were on the improve, houses could be afforded, barbies were becoming popular, people had thrown off their war-time blues, and the spectre of impending doom was replaced by the feeling that anything was possible.

A series of four articles was published by an eminent economist from Britain, Barbara Ward. She had travelled and researched extensively here, and her much-read views were widely respected. She argued that Australia was in a unique position in the world, it had emerged from the War in a much better position than any other nation, and had unlimited resources at its disposal. It also had an educated and civilized population quite likely to exploit these resources in a laconic way, and was free from the internal ethnic and racial problems that divided other nations. Even allowing for the big divide between our States and the Commonwealth governments, she expected that we would prosper and grow at a rate that would be the envy of the world. Such an opinion fitted in well with the mood of Australia at the time. Kids born here at the time were off to a good start.

So, after that little primer, we are almost ready to go. First, though, on the next page I have given you a few Rules that I use in writing. They will help you navigate your way through the book.

MY RULES IN WRITING

NOTE. Throughout this book, I rely a lot on reproducing Letters from the newspapers. Whenever I do this, I put the text in a different font, and indent it a little, and make the font somewhat smaller. I do not edit the text at all. That is, I do not correct spelling or grammar, and if the text gets at all garbled, I do not correct it. It's just as it was seen in the Papers.

SECOND NOTE. The material for this book, when it comes from newspapers, is reported as it was seen at the time. If the benefit of hindsight over the years changes things, then I might record that in my Comments. The info reported thus reflects matters as they were seen in 1952.

THIRD NOTE. Let me also apologise in advance to anyone I might offend. In a work such as this, it is certain some people will think I got some things wrong. I am sure that I did, but please remember, all of this is only my opinion. And really, my opinion does not matter one little bit in the scheme of things. I hope you will say "silly old bugger", shrug your shoulders, and read on.

So, now we really are ready. Let's go.

JANUARY: CHURCHES UNDER FIRE

During WWII, there had been a noticeable increase in the number of people attending church services, and in the number of people who expressed a belief in the efficacy of prayer. The sermons delivered then, however, were a disappointment to many. Their criticism was that they concentrated on abstract matters like the value of Christian faith and love of God, rather that on matters relating to the War or the dire social consequences of the conflict.

Since the end of the War, attendances had fallen, and it seemed that the community was, more than ever before, moving further and further away from church attendance, and from matters such as strict observance of Sundays.

Letters, like the two below, were becoming more common.

Letters, Mary Abercrombe. I read reports in your paper from last Sunday's church services. **One report** told me that I should be busy in spiritual work and carry the message of God to all and sundry. **A second** said that even the smallest sin is enormous when compared to the perfection of God, and it is only through the mercy of God that we are spared the enternal punishment of Hell, and have the option of a half-way house, in Purgatory.

A third told me that no matter what befalls me, just accept it as part of God's plan for me, and that, by suffering in silence, I would be getting credits in Heaven. I could hear Karl Marx rotating to the cheers of the capitalists.

Whatever are these people talking about? Surely, if you want to be a Christian in this world, you need to address **issues that confront us in our real world**.

I would like some sensible guidance on the right attutude to the war in Korea. Should we be killing our own boys and theirs? If so, to what purpose? Should we be taking their orphaned children? Of course you would say we should, but give me three goood reasons why.

Should my husband disobey a strike order from a Communist? If he does not, then he will be branded a scab. What do we do then? Should workers accept their lot, and build up their heavenly credits, or should they speak out and act out?

It is these issues and dozens of others that need discussion from the pulpit. Not **orders** from the pulpit, but rather a sensible discussion from the pulpit. With pros and cons, and then maybe the position of the church at the end.

Spare us from the love of God and his infinite benevolence rubbish while it is obvious that it is from him that all the problems originate.

Letters, Likely Agnostic.   Most churches work on a three year calender. This mean that if they want to tell us about the prodigal son, we will hear about him now, and then three years later. Every Sunday has its sermon already decided three years in advance. That means too that the subject matter is decided and **ossified**.

There is no room for the clergy to regularly get up on Sundays and talk about issues and problems and decisions of the day. Should we **refuse** to trade with Red China even if we need the money? What about if they are in a famine? Should we then let them starve? Is that the way that Christians should behave?

Should we love the Japanese who committed their atocities on us so recently? It is a crime or a sin for a father of four to steal bread from a shop when he has no money at all and is living in a disused chookshed?

We can get the secular view from many sources, but our clergy remain silent. Are they so loocked up with their Bibles that they can't have opinions on current affairs?

Are they frightened that if they put the Christian view, without hiding behind out-of-place quotes from the Bible, that they would be laughed to scorn?

SUNDAY MOVIES

Sunday movies were growing in popularity. Last year in Sydney, they had been allowed in the city, but were **required to show pictures of high moral values**. But gradually, that value was getting more dubious, and there were cries to allow the movies to be shown elsewhere. This Letter below is typical of the many that criticised these proposed changes.

Letters, Christopher Storrs, Bishopsholme, Grafton. Sunday is a day which, in our history, has been **invaluable in maintaining security and balance among people**, giving to many a pause for recollection and worship, opportunities for family and social life, and a weekly reminder that the best recreations and amusements are those devised by ourselves for ourselves, and not those manufactured for us and served up ready-made.

It is a day more needed now than ever as an interruption to routine, in which we can look upward and think, and consider where we are going and at what we are aiming, one on which we can gather spiritual morale for new effort.

It is true that there are always a number of people at a loose end on Sundays in our towns and cities: but "hard cases make bad laws," and for the sake of these people to undermine our Anglo-Saxon Sunday would be progress backwards. Gloom, as you say, is not piety! But neither is the glamour of the footlights synonymous with light-heartedness and refreshment of spirit!

I believe that, if this decadent step is given, there will be deep dismay among all who believe that the greatness of Australia is bound up with the faith and Church of Christ, and who are convinced that the distinctiveness of Sunday has been providentially given to us, and that it cannot be drastically tampered with without **grave hurt to the solidity and depth of Australian character**.

CAPITAL PUNISHMENT

The issue of capital punishment **for murder** was always lurking in the background. Most States still allowed it, and Victoria was still prepared to use it, in the case of Jean Lee in 1951. Recently, in NSW, the case of a Mr Frederick McDermott who had been sentenced to death four years ago was re-examined, with the result that his guilty verdict was quashed. He was released from detention, and compensation was being considered. Predictably, this raised again the arguments against execution of offenders, and some of it is shown below.

Letters, Vernon Treatt, Legislative Assembly. Alderman Albert W Thompson's letter on capital punishment in last Saturday's "Sydney Morning Herald" contained a serious misstatement of fact as to what would be the attitude of a NSW **Liberal** Government in respect of capital offences.

Mr Thompson, using the McDermott case in support of his advocacy of the abolition of capital punishment, states that McDermott was sentenced to death and

"Had it not been that a change of government occurred shortly afterward, a guiltless individual would today.... have been mouldering in his felon's grave..."

The implication of Mr Thompson's words clearly is that, when a prisoner is sentenced to death, this sentence is, under a Liberal Government, automatically carried out. This is completely incorrect.

The fact that a Labour Government **always** refuses to carry out the death penalty may have led Alderman Thompson into thinking (and stating), quite wrongly, that a Liberal Government **always** enforces it.

The true position is that on a conviction for murder, all the facts, including the summing up of the Trial Judge, the nature and circumstances surrounding the commission of the crime, and the moral guilt of the accused would be considered by a Liberal Government.

Where the Crown's case is based on weak circumstantial evidence, or where there are extenuating circumstances, **a Liberal Government** would take the necessary steps to see that **the prerogative of mercy is exercised** and the death sentence commuted to one of imprisonment.

There is absolutely no justification for the categorical statement that, had a Liberal government been in power, the capital punishment imposed on Frederick McDermott would have been carried out.

Letters, A Chisholm, The Australian Encyclopaedia, Editor. Certain misconceptions appear to have arisen over the Australian **political** attitude to capital punishment.

It is, of course, wrong to suppose that non-Labour Governments always enforce the death penalty, and it is also wrong to suppose that Labour Governments always commute such a sentence.

Records of "The Australian Encyclopaedia" reveal that **six executions for capital offences have taken**

place under Labour Ministries in Western Australia, and that Labour governments in South Australia and Tasmania have also carried the death sentence into effect.

Comment. Capital punishment as a threat was kept on the statute books for the States for decades to come. The last such execution was of a Robert Ryan in Victoria, in 1967. After that, in Victoria, South Australia and Western Australia, occasional death sentences were issued, but **all were commuted to life imprisonment.** Western Australia was the last state to remove it for murder in 1984. In NSW, treason, **piracy** and arson of naval dockyards was removed from its ambit in 1985. **In 2010, Federal Legislation prohibited the death penalty for all States and Territories.**

ROYAL TOUR IS COMING SOON

The Federal Minister-in-Charge of the upcoming Royal Tour of Australia announced today that the royal couple, Princess Elizabeth and Prince Phillip would arrive in sunny Sydney on April 1st. That day would be proclaimed a public holiday in Sydney. Three new postage stamps had been commissioned for the occasion. The first of these would carry the head of Elizabeth alone, while the other two would present the royal couple together.

This was something to look forward to. As a spectacle, Royal Tours had always been good fun, and this one, in these auspicious times, promised to be brilliant. So, in a population that still revered the monarchy, there was much good-natured commentary on the pleasing prospect likely.

News item, Jan 14. Formal dress will not be compulsory for Australians who attend official functions during the visit of Princess Elizabeth and the Duke of Edinburgh.

The Minister in Charge of the Royal tour, Mr Eric Harrison said today that it was the wish of the King and of Princess Elizabeth and the Duke of Edinburgh that Australians should not stay away from any function to which they had been invited because they did not possess formal dress.

"It is their Royal Highnesses' wish that no one shall feel obliged to incur the expense of buying formal clothes, which they do not normally wear," said Mr Harrison.

"On appropriate occasions, the Duke of Edinburgh will probably wear morning dress (top hat and morning coat), lounge suit (with soft hat), evening suit (white tie and tails), and dinner jackets (soft shirt and soft collar). Male members of the Royal household will wear similar dress.

"At such functions as garden parties, Australians should feel free to wear either a morning coat or a lounge suit," said Mr Harrison. "Similarly, anyone who is unable to attend a large evening party in a white tie and tail coat should wear a dinner jacket. Those who do not have a dinner jacket should **not** stay away on that account, but could wear a dark blue suit."

Inevitably, not everyone was happy.

Letters, Churchill Avern. As one who has had some experience of lying in hospital whilst the rest of the world passes by and celebrates, I add my support to the remarks of Mr Blake Pelly concerning the omission of the Repatriation General Hospital, Concord, from the itinerary of the Royal tour.

Whilst recognising the heavy demands on the Royal couple and the fact that not everyone can be satisfied, I am sure that they are the first who would wish to make some gesture to incapacitated ex-Servicemen. A visit to Concord, as representative of all such institutions, would provide an occasion for such a gesture.

With two such champions of the cause of Servicemen as Mr Harrison and Lieutenant-General Berryman at the head of the Royal tour, one wonders how such an omission came to be made or who was responsible for the decision.

Letters, Leo G Rowe. May I suggest that in preparation for the Royal visit, the pylons of the Sydney Harbour Bridge, also all other masonry connected with the Bridge, be washed down or steam-cleaned to remove the rust stains and other grime which makes them look so shabby and neglected.

I feel certain that on arrival in Sydney one of the first things her Royal Highness will do will be to view the Bridge. It is to be hoped she will be able to see it as it was designed to appear.

Letters, F M Cowper. Apropos of the wish expressed by Mr Rowe, I have been waiting a long time for someone to raise the question as to why the unsightly concrete military pill-boxes have not been removed from the tops of the pylons on the Harbour Bridge. These pill-boxes were erected during the war and completely ruin the admirable proportions of the pylons as originally designed by the London architects, Sir John Burnett, Tait and Lorne.

If the amount of time and care taken to arrive at these proportions is considered and when it is realised that the bridge is probably the most photographed and widely publicised single feature of Sydney, it does not speak very highly of the aesthetic perceptions of those responsible, for allowing such ugly excrescences to remain to shame us.

Comment. I have the feeling that as we get closer to the happy occasion, there will be even more equally momentous Letters to keep us all on our toes.

ATTITUDE TO FOREIGNERS

The War had finished in 1945. In 1952 we were just seven years away from the cessation of hostilities. The wounds left by the War were deep, the hatreds bred then were still strong in many people, and in some people who had suffered great loss, the scars would never heal.

So, while there was a growing feeling in the community that we should get about our own business, and forgive our former enemies, this was by no means universal, nor was it consistent within any one person.

This uncertainty is reflected in the correspondence below.

Letters, Francis Everingham. There have been many disquieting references in recent weeks to Japan, its people, industries and future.

Is it necessary to seek Japanese friendship or trade on the spurious and wicked grounds that in the event of war they will fight on our side against a possible aggressor nation? Is it not more likely that they will ally themselves with the Asiatic bloc, if armed, in the undoubted belief that their superiority in technical achievement will allow them to rise and grasp the prizes of "Pan-Asian prosperity" they so nearly achieved in World War II?

News item, Jan 20. The Minister for Immigration, Mr H Holt, today appealed to Australians to treat Asians who were temporarily resident in Australia with friendliness.

Addressing the Australian Citizenship Convention, Mr Holt revealed that at present there are about 1,800 Asian students in Australia.

He said Australia was earning goodwill throughout Asia as a result of the happy letters written by students to their relatives and friends at home. Parents who had visited their children in the course of their studies had been relieved to find an absence of any discrimination against them.

Press item, Jan 31. The Consul-General for Greece, Mr E Vrisakis, said last night he hoped to see the Minister for Immigration, Mr Harold Holt, to try to get an immigration agreement similar to that with the Italian Government. "We do not ask for preferential treatment, but we think **we should be treated as well as our former enemies, the Italians,**" he said. "Many Greeks, who have relatives in Australia, are finding difficulty in coming here. Italians, **under the assisted passages scheme**, have their fare paid by the two Governments.

"Shipping is provided for the Italians, but the Greeks have to make their own arrangements. Unlike the Italians, the Greeks must have 50 Pounds sterling or must be guaranteed by their relatives and have accommodation and jobs set up."

Comment. In the War, **Italy was our sworn enemy, and Greece was truly our great ally.** Going on this Letter, it seems pretty tough on the Greeks.

FEBRUARY: THE COMING ROYAL TOUR

Enthusiasm for Elizabeth's visit continued to grow. It seemed that there were people everywhere who wanted their own patch of Australia to share in the royal patronage. Kurnell, on Botany Bay, the place where Governor Phillip first set foot ashore, was pushing for inclusion in the intinerary.

Letters, James W Mackrell, Kurnell Progress Association. Now that the visit of Princess Elizabeth and the Duke of Edinburgh is close, we would like to draw public attention to the omission of Kurnell, the birthplace of Australia, from the itinerary of the tour.

We feel that it would be most appropriate for the Royal couple to be shown this historic spot. The recent re-enactment of the Landing could be repeated at little cost. With the support of the Navy this could be made an event which would live in memory.

This was not universally popular.

Letter, Tom Pride. Kurnell is a run-down small suburb of Sydney, fit only for oil terminals. There is nothing there except for a small commemorative plaque, and I am sure the Royal couple will not want to see something as boring. If they do, they can go look at Nelson's Column. They cannot be asked to go to every little boring place in Australia. Their tour should be planned, not to satisfy local residents, but to give them a relaxed and carefree holiday that they will remember as such for the rest of their lives.

Still, many hearts in Australia were stirred by feelings of glee and goodwill towards the Royal family and Elizabeth. The Editorial from the *Sydney Morning Herald* (*SMH*) **laid it on pretty thick**, yet it truly spoke for millions of patriots here.

The Editorial, along with other writers, pointed out that England was patron of **a vast Empire** that covered the seven seas. It extended right round the world and that, within the Empire, the monarch can travel to any part and be greeted with happiness by the subjects. It was the single biggest trading bloc and had been for centuries. Its wealth and power were greater now than ever, and **its political and social steadiness were the envy of the world**.

The writers dwelt on the unique place of the Crown in the relationship between the Commonwealth partners, and how it was seen to establish invisible yet binding links between eight major nations and innumerable smaller colonies and dependencies. It has bound together, as no other formal linkage had ever done, countries from the East and the West, rich and poor, developed and developing. It is the tangible symbol of intangible bonds.

The *SMH* extolled "the King and his family, by attracting to themselves, to their simplicity, their dignity and their essential humanity, the personal loyalty of diverse races and creeds in the Commonwealth and Colonies, have made a direct and substantial contribution to the peaceful evolution of Empire."

The writers went on to admire the way in which the young Princess had emulated her parents, and the wholesome and full dedication that she was showing in accepting the tough tasks of touring the world in their stead. But it was obvious to all that her previous conduct throughout her life had already earned her the respect and love of millions of observers all round the world. The Herald concluded "so successful has Princess Elizabeth been in emulating her parents in this that she will be welcomed everywhere less as a personage than as a personality. She holds, indeed, a very special place in the affections of her people. Her growth from childhood to young womanhood has been closely and sympathetically followed by millions who, in the normal course of events, will one day acknowledge her as their Queen. Her ready assumption of responsibilities which rarely fall to one of her sex and age, and her earnest preparation for others yet more exacting, have won hearts the world over."

Party poopers. It seems though that certain **City of Sydney aldermen** were not caught up in the enthusiasm. They decided, in official Caucus, that they **would not wear their official aldermanic robes at receptions** and functions for the Princess. The exception to this decision was the Lord Mayor, Alderman O'Dea, who decided to uphold the dignity of his office by wearing the official robes and gold chains. His robes include a crimson-lined gown edged with ermine. His chain has 49 gold links and three large medallions.

The leader of the opposing Civic Reform Party said he was disappointed with the Caucus decision. He said "all aldermen should do everything possible to uphold their office and add to the colour of the official ceremonies. The Lord Mayor is to be congratulated by showing himself to be big enough to ignore such a silly and petty decision."

NO SHORTAGE OF BLACK-OUTS

In the wonderful picture that Barbara Ward painted of Australia, she forgot to mention that Oz was suffering from endemic blackouts. In most states, in most cities and most country towns, blackouts on a daily basis were just something you had to live with. The problem started in the War years, when maintenance of infrastructure was shelved in favour of the more pressing need for munitions. Since then, money had been short for all types of reconstruction. Power generators were no exception.

In Sydney the shortage of electricity was managed by dividing the city into five Zones. Ideally, each Zone would have blackouts during the peak industrial hours on one day per week. These hours would be announced to the public in advance, so that householders and factories could make appropriate plans. As it turned out, often these best-laid plans went awry, and several Zones were "out" at once, and black-outs were likely at random times. Typically, once the power went off, it stayed off for a couple of hours or more, and all too often, it came back on again for a while and then went off again. Needless to say, quite a few people objected. Households hated it.

In February, the NSW Electricity Commission announced that recent inspections of plant at Sydney's main generator, at Bunnerong, had revealed that many units were badly corroded, and that they would need to be replaced as soon as possible. In the meantime, they would require much maintenance, and that would have to be carried out on week-days. That meant that power output would be reduced on those week-days, and so **rationing in the coming year would be more severe than last year.**

The spokesman went on to say that many factories were now shifting to Saturday production to make up for weekday black-outs, and that meant that, in future, rationing by Zones would be **extended to Saturdays as well.** Politicians were very busy at this time beating their breasts, and pointing out that it that it was all someone else's fault, and that it was a necessary legacy from the past. One Letter-writer had his own views on this.

Letters, Mining Engineer.   I have used boilers in smelters, mines, chemical works, etc., in various parts of the world, and provided ordinary precautions are taken, there is very little deterioration.

In the high pressure boilers of the type at Bunnerong, every possible facility is provided to deal with bad water of every description. If this is done, very little wear will occur. But unless care is taken, a boiler, like every other machine, loses efficiency.

In all plants I have managed, continuity of work was essential, and provision was made for spare boilers, spare electric generators, and spare transformers. A periodic inspection was made by a Government boiler inspector, and the boiler was closed down (hence the installation of a spare), thoroughly examined and tested by water pressure at 30 to 40 per cent higher than the working pressure, as a matter of safety.

This raises the question: have the Bunnerong boilers been carefully tested, and examined as is required at other plants? If so, why have they been allowed to get into the dangerous condition as described, when the damage must have been very gradual in this high class of plant?

Comment. This black-out situation in Sydney, and similar ones elsewhere, took years to fix. During that period, there were many politicians, including Prime Minister Menzies, blaming strikes, and the Communists, for reducing

Australian production. I have seen calculations, however, that appeared to show that **power rationing** across the nation **reduced production much more than strikers ever did.**

NO SLEEP FOR PRISONERS IN CHURCHES

The Church of England got more that its fair share of publicity this month, though it might have preferred not to. A group of semi-professional actors prepared to enact a play by Christopher Fry, called *A Sleep of Prisoners*. This told the story of four British airmen who had been shot down in WWII over enemy France, and who took refuge for days in a cathedral. A good-sized sandstone church was the ideal setting for the play, and the Holy Trinity Church, Milsons Point, in Sydney, was chosen as a good venue. It was planned that an extended season would run there.

The play, which was originally commissioned by the Religious Drama Society of Great Britain, had first been performed last year in St Thomas' Church in London, and had since been presented in hundreds of churches in Britain and the US. It was written by one of Britain's outstanding poets, and is "a plea against violence in human affairs, and a call for hope, patience, and greater striving for goodness in all human conduct."

After the first performance in early February, the Church of England announced that it **would not permit further performances in any of its churches throughout Australia.** The producer, Mr William Orr, announced that the production would be the first and last at Holy Trinity. "Apparently, people in high places in the C of E object to the use of a church for a stage presentation." He added, "You can't blame them. It's **their** church."

Other people were not so sanguine. Criticism was widespread, though moderate, as in the four Letters below.

Letters, Felix Arnott, St Paul's College, University of Sydney. I was present at the first performance of "Sleep of Prisoners" at the Garrison Church last Friday evening, and like most of those in the large congregation, was deeply moved by the sensitive beauty of Christopher Fry's play, which was acted with true understanding and reverence.

The play had been written obviously for performance in a church, and would have lost much of the subtlety of its religious message if performed anywhere else.

Even if certain business arrangements were deemed unsuitable in this particular case, it is sad that in Sydney this play should be denied performance in the manner its most reverent author intended, especially since it has been played to deeply appreciative congregations in Anglican churches in most parts of the world.

It is hard, too, to understand why real drama should be thus banned from its ancient and cherished home, the Christian Church, when musical performances and films are frequently allowed, and these rarely possessing any merit beyond a nauseating sentimentality and a commonplace message. Fortunately, it is only the diocese of Sydney that has banned the play, and we hope that in other parts of the Anglican Communion in the Commonwealth, the gospel for our day in "Sleep of Prisoners" will receive an appreciative welcome.

Letters, Bryson Taylor. A study of the development of English drama shows that our first plays were of a religious character. Performances were given in the sacred buildings themselves; the priests were the actors. Drama was one of its chief factors in the mental and spiritual enlightenment of the people by the medieval Church.

So the banning of Christopher Fry's "A Sleep of Prisoners" written for church presentation, comes as a surprise to those who look to the Church for spiritual and intellectual refreshment.

Many of our city churches with their fine naves and good acoustic properties (notably the church of St Philip, Church Hill) would be ideal for presentation of such plays as "Saint Joan," "Murder in the Cathedral," "Androcles and the Lion."

Some of our churches lie in darkness on week nights when they could be used for enlightenment through suitable drama – such as was the practice in medieval times.

Letters, Richard Aspinall. For long, church leaders have bemoaned dwindling congregations, complained of lack of funds, and castigated parishioners for deserting the churches and their pews.

Now they reprove a young vicar with an unusual approach to these problems by permitting a performance of Christopher Fry's "A Sleep of Prisoners." Had the Archbishop been present in the congregation I feel that he would have found an extreme of "real worship" and, together with all present, been filled with a "sense of awe and reverence."

This play is a means to **crowding every church every night**, extending congregations, spreading further the Church's message and swelling church funds. Religious drama has a long history, and only fear of offending today's small congregations can keep it out of the Church where it belongs. And this fear can cripple the Church forever.

Letters, Ian Hogbin. The Dean of Sydney has said that in no circumstances could a function **involving**

the sale of tickets be held in a church. A symphony orchestra recently gave performances of Bach's works in St Andrew's Cathedral, and members of the congregation were granted admission only on condition that they **bought programmes beforehand**. Are we then to assume that if the rector of St Thomas', Miller's Point, had not taken the course of charging admission and instead sold programmes, the authorities would have allowed him to continue with his season of "A Sleep of Prisoners"?

Further comments. There were a few fireworks still in the offing, from other **unexpected less-moderate sources**. The *SMH*'s Editor was not at all impressed by the ban by the church hierarchy. He wrote of "episcopal narrow-mindedness that has put organised religion on the defence", and of "religious zeal outrunning wisdom", and of having "shown themselves bound by outmoded views on the relations between Church and people."

The Bishop Coadjutor of Sydney, Bishop Hilliard, replied. He opined that there were times when it was **more laudable to be narrow-minded than broad-minded**, and that often the voice of the people was not the word of God. He pointed out that many parishioners supported his ban, and "their feelings and convictions are at least as worthy of administrative consideration as the views of editors and playwrights."

He quoted the incident in the New Testament when our Lord chased the money lenders from the temple, arguing that the temple was a House of Prayer. Given **that**, it was hard to see a church being used as a place of popular entertainment.

The Editor replied. He derided the Bishop's claim that he did not know anything about the play until the eve of the performance. **But if that was indeed so**, then it showed how far out of touch he was with the community he serviced. After all, the plans had been widely reported by the Press, and discussed by the public for weeks before.

He went on to point out that the Bishop had not told the whole story about the incident in the temple. What Jesus denounced was a House of Prayer being made **into a den of thieves**. Was the bishop suggesting that this was what was being done here? The play was a religious one, performed in innumerable churches with episcopal blessing, in England and the US. "Are we to believe that the authorities **there** have less sense of the sacred and spirit of reverence than we have in Sydney?"

It seemed that this matter was far from closed. But it was suddenly dwarfed in significance by a truly tragic and unexpected event of world importance.

DEATH OF GEORGE VI

Shortly before 11am (9pm Sydney time) Buckingham Palace issued this announcement:

"It was announced from Sandringham at 10.45am (8.45pm Sydney time) today, February 6, 1952, that the King who retired to rest last night in his usual health passed peacefully away in his sleep early this morning.

"Staying at Sandringham with the King when he died were the Queen and their younger daughter, Princess Margaret, and the new Queen's two children, Prince Charles and Princess Anne.

"King George VI was 56. He became King on December 11, 1936, with the abdication of his brother King Edward VIII, now the Duke of Windsor. The King had been in ill health frequently during the last four years. He was operated on during September 23 last year for removal of his left lung under circumstances which indicated that he had cancer.

"The reason for the operation was never officially announced. Recent pictures of the King had shown a haggard and tired man. All court functions have been cancelled, but arrangements for the funeral, and for the period of mourning, await the new Queen's return.

"The new Queen's son, Prince Charles, is now the heir to the throne. Her daughter, Princess Anne, is second in succession. Both children at present are at Sandringham. They have not been told of the death as yet. This will be delayed until their parents can do it, and then spend some time with them.

"The King made his last public appearance on January 31st when he farewelled his daughter and her husband at London airport. On that occasion, he stood bareheaded for 30 minutes. This caused Press comment on the wisdom of the King's action, though it was generally accepted as a sign of his good recovery.

"The new Queen is in Kenya, East Africa, and was due to sail from Mombasa tomorrow for Australia and New Zealand. Now she will leave immediately by air for London and is expected to cancel her planned tour."

The news of the death shocked the British nation. Conferences and meetings were cancelled. Law Courts and the Stock Exchange were closed. Sports meetings and horse racing too were cancelled, and theatres were closed. Crowds gathered outside Buckingham Palace, and many women sobbed.

It is clear that **the tour of Australia will sadly be postponed**. Arthur Fadden, our Federal Treasurer, will represent Australia at the official ceremonies, including the King's funeral.

Queen Elizabeth. Comment. Looking back more than 65 years, it seems remarkable that Elizabeth would saddle up to take the job, apparently without any hesitation at all. Granted that she had been groomed all her life to do so. But for a young woman, to take on such an onerous task, every day for the rest of her life, was promising a lot. Which, I am delighted to say, has been honoured to this very day.

Letters, R G Casey, Melbourne. In an address at the Wesley Church in Melbourne on Sunday last, I suggested that the accession of the young Queen might well have a profound effect on the attitude of mind of all her many peoples. Perhaps I might enlarge on this view.

A young, happily married woman with a young family has suddenly become the constitutional head of all this great and widespread Commonwealth of peoples. The great preoccupation with public affairs that this great responsibility entails will engage all her efforts and energies for all of her life, to the practical exclusion of any degree of carefree existence that any young human being might reasonably expect to look forward to.

I believe that these facts will impress themselves on the minds of countless people. They will realise that things have not been going too well lately – and that a great burden of public affairs has now fallen on the shoulders of a young woman.

Many people will tend to ask themselves if it is fair and right that such a young woman should be required to give everything in the public interest while vast numbers of her people give much less. If she uncomplainingly takes on an inhumanly difficult and exacting burden, should not the rest of us at least do our utmost in our daily lives and work?

If we were all to decide to share the burden with the young Queen, we would start a chain reaction that might well have most remarkable results. I ask myself if we can, in decency, do any less.

Letters, Mary Hill. I was much impressed by Mr R G Casey's fine letter, and have thought much of how we might help to realise his hopes.

There might be some small remedy for the apathy and disinclination toward work if the housewife could readjust her attitude to work in the home.

There is **a habit today of bemoaning the lot of the housewife**, her ills and hardships, and of bringing forth all manner of labour-saving devices as a panacea. Women are being slowly convinced that their life is composed chiefly of hardships and drudgery. Yet I am sure – my own case being surely typical of thousands – that few of us would change our position if given the opportunity.

Stressing the burden of work can only give growing children the impression that work is something unpleasant, and to be avoided wherever possible. Whereas surely it has been proved throughout the history of the world that **the only real happiness and fulfillment is in work**.

As an example (whether we like it or not) to future Australian citizens, we might do much to alter this half-hearted approach to life, by taking as an inspiration the unquestioning devotion to unceasing work and duty as shown us already by our young Queen Elizabeth II.

NEWS AND VIEWS

Letters, Mrs Ruth Baker. May I pass comment on the uninteresting variety of cakes presented to city housewives by the pastrycooks?

Year in and year out it is possible to see the same cakes in the same position in the windows. Yet, with so many lovely recipe books about, we are still offered sickly mock cream, the good old block cake, and pies in all forms, apple, mince, and meat.

I object to paying fourpence each for unsold cakes wrapped up in coconut and called lamingtons.

Letters, D Sharland. However monotonous the cakes sold in Sydney may be, as your correspondents assert, they could not be more so than (with a few exceptions) our fruit and vegetable salads.

Most restaurants nowadays are sufficiently daring to add grated carrot to the usual salad of lettuce, tomato, and cooked beetroot, but other vegetables are equally gratable.

And with our splendid variety of fruit, why are we so often offered the **fruit salad** of orange, apple, and banana, sometimes tinned? With nothing else added?

MARCH: BOB IS NOT YOUR UNCLE

For the last few months, Australia's major trading partners had been feeling the economic pinch. America was well and truly sick of the Korean war, and her military spending had been cut back from earlier higher levels. Britain was spending many more Pounds than she earned, and in early March indicated that she intended to bring in all sorts of restrictions on overseas spending. Not surprisingly, the Australian Government thought it was a good time to take stock of our own situation, and when they did, they found that we too were in a parlous situation.

Prime Minister Bob Menzies first broached this a few times in early March, much to the surprise of everyone, who had been constantly assured that everything was hunky dory. He ominously issued a series of **vague threats** that puzzled and alarmed the nation. "We have been moving of late into **a giant economic crisis**. Before we are much older we may have to experience far-reaching changes in our financial position. **I can't go into details**, but you will know about them before you are much older. They will involve enormous difficulties and problems, but I think all those who believe in the Government will realise that we don't adopt policies **without the most careful study and thought." Very mysterious.**

Within a week, his heavy-handed vagueness gave way to two definite measures, which were obviously introduced **without** the slightest suggestion of careful study or thought. **In the first measure**, the Commonwealth Bank, acting on the Government's behalf, said that import licenses would be introduced on anyone who wanted to import anything from Britain, Europe, or America. Such regulations had been relaxed in the few years following the War, and importers had grown accustomed to more-or-less freely ordering from overseas, without consulting Government.

On top of that, it said that **the quantity of goods** allowed into Oz would be reduced. The cuts were massive. Some goods were cut by 80 per cent. Items thus affected included textiles, cigarettes, spirits, car bodies, motor cycles and refrigerators. Those in the 40 per cent bracket included iron and steel pipes and barbed wire. Too bad if you were a farmer. No decision had yet been made about raw materials and petrol. It proved to be the case that almost all goods were subject to cuts of these magnitudes.

Now, however, whether you or a company wanted to import anything, from toothbrushes to cars to clothing, you would need to get permission from reluctant Government agencies. Further, the very purpose of imposing the restrictions was to reduce imports, so that it was certain that many applications would be refused. But **only after the request had been duly considered for weeks or months by an agency that was yet to be created.**

Businesses rightly immediately claimed that the rationing of imports would surely shut them down, and the uncertainty and delay would finish off anyone who survived. In fact, for many, this proved to be the case.

In the second measure, the Bank also announced that Oz visitors **to** Britain could take only 500 Pounds Sterling with them. If they also went to Europe, the amount was increased to the grand figure of 600 Pounds. Travel industry spokesmen were aghast at this sum. They pointed out that, in 1952, travelers to Britain were inclined to see **their overseas jaunt as a trip of a lifetime**. Generally they went for months, and dived back and forth across the Channel many times, and visited resorts and tourist locations all over Britain. There was no hope that Oz tourists could now live out their travel dreams. "The restrictions will cause wholesale cancellations of passages to England by people who will be unable to fulfill their holiday plans on the meager 500 Pounds allowed to them."

The *SMH* editor expressed clearly the indignation of all sections of the community. Commenting on import restrictions, he said "Consternation and confusion are the first reactions to the staggering import cuts announced at the week-end. The public had no reason to expect anything approaching the severity of these regulations." He went on to say that the move was in stark contrast with the Government's previous line, and was clearly a knee-jerk reaction to events overseas and a lack of foresight at home.

The Letter below voices a typical reactive complaint.

Letters, **R Hartwell, NSW University of Technology.**
As an individual with interests in general reading, as a lecturer with a need for learned books and texts, and as a writer, I protest about the proposed 40 per cent cut in the importation into Australia of British books and magazines.

Cultural activities in Australia are often attacked (for example, by the censors), but never before has the main source of our reading been so seriously threatened. Even during the war, no such restrictions were imposed. The proposed cut may have some economic justification – I doubt it – but it must nevertheless be condemned as an effective attack on our cultural standards. The loss in books which will result cannot be compensated for by increased domestic book production. In particular, universities and other learned institutions will suffer grievously. (About 90 per cent of the books used in universities come from abroad.)

I do not base this protest, however, merely on the interests of universities; it is equally important that the community as a whole is not deprived of its reading. The loss to the general reading public will be enormous.

Many other Letter-writers spoke up. Tom Watters complained that he wanted to buy a piano for his daughter. He would have **none** to choose from, he thought. In the unlikely event that a piano industry started up **here**, he would not trust it, and anyway, it would take too long to be of use to him. Helen Olsen bemoaned that her favorite pickled onions from Wales would not be available. Robert Dole would be denied the goods he needed for his Manchester business. Mark Moon would not be able to take a six-week cruise he had planned in the Mediterranean.

There was only one *SMH* writer who dared to write in favour the regulation.

Letters, Fairplay. The reaction to the Federal Government's protective measures by certain leaders of industry prompts me to appeal for sanity rather than "panic-squealing."

Can the Government be blamed for the enormous imports of the past year? Has not Australian industry failed to produce? Despite appeals even from sane trade-union and labour leaders for increased production, most Australian products – from housing materials to foodstuffs – have been in short supply, and in many cases, on quota. As a result, orders were placed overseas to overcome these shortages. Prices of overseas qualities were considerably higher and the Government, realising our drift towards inflation, introduced credit restriction, and has now imposed import control.

What a spate of unfair criticism has been expressed! As a large importer, I consider that the Government has been wise. There is little doubt that goods which can be proved to have been on firm order when the action was taken will be duly licensed and allowed to enter the country. Let us be sensible and applaud, not censure, the Government for the only sane action it could have taken.

Comment. There is no doubt that these measures were caused by just plain panic in the Government. They were draconian on the one hand, **and** not at all thought out on the other **and**, on the third hand, worked contrary to the current national objective of controlling inflation. It was just as well for Prime Minister Menzies, and his merry men, that elections were two years away.

BOOK BORROWING

In writing these books, I have found that every now and then a simple, innocent-looking Letter is printed in one of the Papers and seems barely worthy of publication, but which, surprisingly, unleashes all sorts of passions and ideas in the hearts of readers. One such Letter is shown below.

Letters, Bibliophile. I have always had a good library and been in the habit of lending books freely among my friends. I consider myself fortunate if one out of every five lent ever comes back. I have lost more than 1,500 good books over the years.

Can any of your readers suggest some means by which one's books can be lent with a reasonable expectation of their being returned? My name and address are written on the first page of every book; this does not make any difference.

What I think happens mostly is that our friends, after reading the book, place it among their own books. Some of their friends borrow it, and that is the end of it. It would seem a simple matter for them to have a section in their bookshelves for borrowed books not to be re-lent, at least without the owner's consent.

I once thought of putting a red cover around the book with a device like there used to be, in large letters, on all the towels at the old Manly baths many years ago – "Stolen from Stennett's Baths."

I was at a friend's house in Manly a while ago and asked him if he would lend me a book to read. On going through his shelves I found twelve of my own books, some of which had been lent 10 years before. The peculiar fact is that if one lends a lawn mower or an electric iron or a pound of tea, or almost any other article, it is returned, but you seldom see a book again. This causes of a lot of exasperation, and in which no lack of integrity is suggested, but sheer want of method.

The responses came in thick and fast. I have presented some of them below.

Letters, Aristo. Having read Bibliophiles's Letter, I have bought a dozen extra copies of the "*Herald*," from each of which I have clipped his letter. Pasted to appropriately sized pieces of pasteboard, they will serve me as bookmarks to be inserted in every volume in future lent to friends.

Letters, Guilty, Sydney. What a pity "Bibliophile" did not put his real name at the foot of his letter! All his acquaintances would promptly have turned out their bookshelves and he would probably have had every one of his 1,500 lost books returned!

A friend asked me, quite recently, about a book she had lent me. I turned out my bookcase and found four, carefully put away to prevent them being handled, and then forgotten. And yet she lent me another.

Letters, J Douglass. Get a notebook and enter the book when it is handed out, with the date – and tick it off when returned. It might be as well to get the borrower to sign for the book.

I have a strong book sense, with many favourites I should hate to lose. I have often, when asked for the loan of a book, bought a copy and given it away forthright rather than risk its damage.

Letters, D O'B Moate. Bibliophile should get a **bookplate with his name inscribed thereon**, and cease defiling the fly-leaf with, as he says, his name and address. There are many fine bookplate artists in Australia.

A book owner takes a heavy responsibility upon himself when he inscribes his signature to a newly acquired book, maybe even upon the title page that has given the author and his associates so much trouble to fashion and balance to a nicety. Only celebrities are accorded that privilege, and even then the signature is no longer such – it has become an autograph.

Letters, Bruce Rainsford. I am amazed to see that, although he lends his books, "Bibliophile" still has a good library. In borrowing other people's books he is providing the ammunition with which his book-loving (and retaining) friends shoot him. The easiest way to lose both books and friends is to lend the former to the latter.

Letters, Marion Coleman. There is only one thing to do if you must lend your treasured volumes. Note the name of borrower in her presence, and after a while suggest that you would like your books returned.

If you lose a friend, maybe that is preferable to losing – as I have done – irreplaceable autographed copies. If you are not prepared to thus safeguard your property, then do not lend. Be firm.

Letters, JCL. Why all this fuss about losing loaned books? Book lending and borrowing is healthy, sensible, and thrifty. As long as one has the commonsense to acquire as often as he surrenders, then his library will constantly refresh itself at little or no cost.

Few books, once read, are worth keeping. Of about 1,000 volumes in my possession today, I would happily exchange all but a score for fresh books of similar interest. **The miserly retention of books is a vice.**

Letters, (Archdeacon) R Robinson. The Archdeacon Hammond once placed as the Weekly Message on the notice-board outside St Barnabas' Church, George Street West, the following: "Bookkeeping is the art of not returning borrowed books." I believe that, as a result, not a few people had books they had loaned returned to them.

Letters, D Hewlett. "Bibliophile" has my deepest sympathy. My father suffered from the same trouble, but managed to cut the loss of his books to a negligible amount. Under his name and address was written: "It is far more blessed to give than to lend, and it costs about the same." The books always came back.

Letters, W Kett. The problem of forgetful book borrowers is as old as the papyrus and clay tablet.

Ashurbanipal, King of Assyria (BC 668-626), reputed to have possessed a library of 30,000 tablets, experienced the problem, and invoked his gods to no effect. His bookmark bore this imprecation: "Whoso shall carry off this tablet may Ashur and Belit overthrow him in wrath...and destroy his name and posterity from the land."

Letters, H S B. To those who lend books I would suggest: Try writing your name and address at the end of the book – on the page where the story finishes.

Comment. What a great range of opinions on what seemed a simple subject. In the days before TV, holding and lending books from private libraries was much more common than it is today. It was obviously a serious business.

GIESEKING: SUPPORTER OF HITLER?

Walter Gieseking was born in Germany in 1895 of German parents. He served in WWI as a bandsman and later, as a gifted pianist, gave his first performance in London in 1923. During WWII, he continued to live in Germany, and gave a number of concerts there and in German-occupied territories.

After the War, he was accused of being a strong German collaborator, but **was cleared of the charge by the US Military** Government in 1947. In 1949 his tour of America was cancelled after demonstrations marred his performances. However, he continued his tours to many other countries, and returned to the US for a highly successful tour in 1953.

In March, he was scheduled to perform Melbourne and Sydney. On arrival at Melbourne, he was subjected to small, vigorous demonstrations that threatened to cancel his tour. He carried on, however, and his concerts were great successes in both locations.

The protestors were by a small Jewish minority who felt that Gieseking had given war-time support to the Hitler regime, and that he was a party to the persecution of the Jews. The Letters below relate to the Melbourne demos.

Letters, Charles Moses, Chairman of the ABC.

I feel that I must express my disgust at the public insult offered in Melbourne to the distinguished German pianist, Walter Gieseking, by the so-called Jewish Council to Combat Fascism and Anti-Semitism, which organisation has threatened similar action in Sydney next week.

World War II was fought to uphold the rights of free men and to rid the world of racial discrimination and intolerance. Now we see these very ugly symptoms appearing in Australia, and being demonstrated by a minority of the very people who appeal loudest against German discrimination.

The Melbourne demonstrators against Gieseking were not the Christian victims of German aggression - the Poles, Czechs, Norwegians, Dutch, or British. These people have already in many cases welcomed famous artists from Germany who have visited their countries since the war.

I have many good friends of the Jewish faith who will be among the first to deplore the action of the Melbourne demonstrators. They realise that if ever anti-Semitism were to appear in our country – a terrible thought – it would do so solely because of the aggressive, intolerant un-Australian actions of this noisy minority of their fellow Jews.

The ABC has positive evidence that Gieseking was never a Nazi, nor was he ever actively associated with any Nazi organization. He played the piano during the war in Sweden, Switzerland, and even Turkey, as well as in Germany. The fact that his parents were Germans is not his fault, nor is it a reason for insulting an artist of world standing.

I write as one who knows the background of the engagement of Gieseking and who felt impelled to protest at the action of the very small, but noisy and vindictive, section who demonstrated against him and who are trying to organise a boycott of his concerts.

Letters, Saul Symonds, President, NSW Jewish Board of Deputies, Sydney. In his attempt to involve the Jewish community in the ill-conceived demonstrations against Walter Gieseking, Mr Charles Moses has departed from the standard of objectivity to be desired in the general manager of a great public utility.

The ABC claims to have positive evidence that Gieseking was never actively associated with any Nazi organization. It would doubtless interest Mr Moses to know that, as early as November, 1933, Gieseking made active efforts to joint the "Militant League for German Culture" which was the Goebbels-created organisation for Nazi artists and musicians. Indeed, writing to the League in that month, Gieseking said: "I received...a request for payment of back dues...since the money is in any case well spent, I shall pay anyhow."

Furthermore, it has been publicly claimed and never refuted that, whether himself a Nazi or not, Gieseking was a friend of the top-ranking party leaders and played for them all, including Hitler and Mussolini. Contrast this with the attitude of Toscanini who, rather than work amongst the enemies of democracy, went in voluntary exile from his homeland.

Surely Mr Moses is well aware of the fact that Gieseking, who was on the black list of the US Army in 1945, but was whitewashed in 1947, nevertheless, when he visited the USA in 1949, refused to submit to an inquiry into his alleged relations with the Nazis by the US Immigration Department and hurriedly left the country, cancelling his concert tour.

The official bodies of Australian Jewry, Federal and State, issued no statement in regard to Gieseking beyond a suggestion, in one case, that Jews might regard it as a matter of self-respect not be associated with his tour. If a handful of demonstrators, not by any means all Jewish, disregard this passive attitude and indulge in clamorous protest, this seems no justification for the attitude adopted by Mr Moses and the many hurtful remarks in his letter.

Letters, S W Krieger, General Secretary, Association of New Citizens, Sydney. We are not rejecting Gieseking because he is a German, a Christian, an outstanding pianist. Yet we do reject him because he has – despite protestations to the contrary – made himself a willing tool of Nazi "Kultur Propaganda," because he stood by passively while thousands of his fellow artists were shipped to the gas chambers, because he heiled Hitler and fawned to his henchmen.

We challenge Mr Moses or Mr Gieseking to prove the contrary, rather than sidetrack the issue by implying that Gieseking is merely rejected for nationalistic reasons or for economic jealousy between Christians and Jews.

We new citizens deplore the ABC's disregard for the feelings of a section of the public to whom Australia's musical development owes so much.

We do not approve of rowdy demonstrations wherever they originate. We are of the opinion that it can safely be left to the discretion of the individual to decide on dignified expressions of protest.

Letters, Music-Lover. After Hitler had come to power in Germany and before he marched into Austria – i.e. between 1933 and 1938 – Herr Gieseking was heard occasionally in Vienna, but never in the ordinary type of concerts like all the other international artists. He always appeared in a series of concerts arranged and run by Austria's musical "fifth column". Such concerts were scrupulously screened. "Aryan" musicians played for "Aryan" audiences.

On the other hand, it appears inconceivable that anyone condemning German Nazi methods could approve of Nazi methods when practiced by our local Jewish fanatics.

Letters, Louise Cook. Mr Krieger condemns Gieseking "because he stood by passively whilst thousands of his fellow artists were shipped to the gas chambers." The existence of the gas chambers was unknown to the bulk of German people, and if Gieseking is to be condemned for doing nothing about something of which he was not aware, then every other German alive at that time is in the same position.

Letters, Lindley Evans, and others, NSW State Conservatorium of Music, Sydney. We who signed wish to state that we shall welcome with enthusiasm the visit to Sydney of Mr Gieseking, for long recognised as one of the world' great pianists.

Letters, Raymond Fisher. There is not the slightest case for the questioning of the political morals of any artist brought here for a brief tour.

Gieseking has come to play the piano; attendance or non-attendance at his concerts should rest entirely upon one's opinion of him solely as a pianist, and any other consideration is irrelevant.

Comment. It was only 7 years since the end of WWII, and there was no way that everyone had forgotten and forgiven. It seems to me, in my innocence, that during the War Mr Gieseking had been put in an extremely difficult position, and I have no doubt that he made perfectly correct decisions as he saw them at the time. Perhaps he might have changed some of them if he had the benefit of hindsight. But, like most of us, he did not.

Likewise the protestors, presumably still **suffering from the loss of family** in Hitler's death camps, might have acted differently if they had given the matter more thought. But at the time, some of these sufferers would have **welcomed any chance at all to make a public stance** against any part of the Hitler regime. Here was a rare chance to be publicly heard. Nowadays we might call it a part of the healing process.

Readers who are interested in the questions raised here should get a movie film, starring Harvey Keitel, *"Taking Sides"* from their local video store. It covers this issue in poignant detail.

NEWS AND VIEWS

Letters, Apodictic. In an increasing number of shops, evasions of the controlled price of bread are being practised.

A few poppy seeds topping a loaf enable sellers to obtain an increase of price from 5½d (legal price) to 1/3. A fractional addition of milk in baking also causes a similar increase in price. There are unjustified excuses for charging higher for other varieties.

Surely the Government should act promptly to put a stop to this comparatively new exploitation of a most necessary food.

APRIL: A-BOMBS AT MONTE BELLO

Prime Minister Bob Menzies was very keen for Australia to get an atom bomb for defence purposes. Both he and Britain had been lobbying in the US for permission to join with the US and Canada in their so-called "Atom Club." But their efforts had so far been in vain with the US saying that Britain was a security problem, and that Australia could contribute nothing to any arrangement made.

Now, in 1952, Britain was proposing to explode atomic bombs all by itself. Menzies was hoping to get access to some secrets from those explosions, and so had offered Woomera in South Australia as a site for the tests. This meant that Britain would begin testing here in a few months.

But Menzies was not finished yet. On April 1st, he announced that Australia was now prepared to mine and sell uranium from a new discovery at Radium Hill, also in South Australia. The two lucky countries who were deemed worthy of receiving this precious and scarce commodities were, not surprisingly, the US and Britain. Surely, it seemed, **wrongly**, that these nations would be so grateful to us that they would cough up at least some of their secrets.

So we started our long and chequered history of exporting, and not exporting, uranium to the rest of the world. That in turn started the ongoing debates about whether we should mine this potentially dangerous material. Over the years, we have argued ourselves to exhaustion over whether we should export it to anyone, and whether we should use it for our own energy needs, and how we should transport our waste materials, and how we should we dispose of them. The range of still-unsettled arguments about uranium has only grown since 1952, and it appears that a consensus or even a consistent national policy is a long way off. Letter-writers in 1952 raised arguments that were very different from those today.

Letters, D Mellor, Chemistry Department, University of Sydney. Our mineral resources are a wasting asset. Once used they can never be replaced.

It is not suggested that we should hoard our uranium, since to adopt such a dog-in-the-manger attitude of refusing to supply the USA, with whom we have a defensive alliance, would be the height of folly. There are, however, different forms in which uranium could be supplied. We could, for example, export the crude **or the partly concentrated ores**.

We should try to take advantage of what appears to be a golden opportunity for developing the technique of extracting, from the ores, **pure uranium compounds and metallic uranium itself**, if necessary. Better still, though this would be a great deal more difficult to achieve, we might attempt to process the ores for Uranium 235 or plutonium and export either of these substances in strictly controlled amounts.

Even if, by trading uranium for "know how" and equipment instead of dollars, we can only develop the technology as far as the extraction of pure compounds and metallic uranium, we shall be in a far better position than we otherwise would be to take advantage of our irreplaceable uranium resources when the day of industrial atomic power arrives, as it surely will.

At all costs we should avoid exhausting our resources before that day arrives. We are posterity's keeper.

Letters, A Penfold, F Morrison, Museum of Applied Arts and Sciences. We concur in Dr Mellor's opinion that our precious deposits of uranium should be conserved. We should in no circumstances export the ore, but undertake the processing of it here, and permit the export of Uranium 235 or plutonium in strictly controlled amounts.

The United States of America and the United Kingdom are not desperately short of uranium. They are able to obtain their requirements of uranium from the deposits of the Congo, Canada and Colorado.

The use of uranium as a source of power need not be deferred for 10 years if we apply ourselves as assiduously to that problem as we do to its use for military purposes. It is quite possible that the period could be shortened to five years or even less.

In view of the deteriorating situation with regard to **coal supplies**, we should look ahead and realise that uranium may be substituted for coal in our power plants when it becomes feasible to release it in the form of electrical power, notwithstanding the fact that there is the question of relative costs to be considered.

There is another factor – **that of public health** – which should ensure the highest priority being given to the problem of using uranium as a source of industrial and domestic energy. A leading medical authority in the United Kingdom has just pointed out that the inhalation of power-station smoke dust killed many more people in 1949 than did accidents of all types and causes.

This raises the question of the probably deleterious action of the black and white smoke particles which are released daily in great volumes from the power stations of Sydney. This serious hazard to public health does not appear to have received the attention it merits. It is a national problem. Therefore, it offers one particularly good and urgent reason why a special effort should be made to develop our uranium resources for ultimate use as electrical power.

Comment. Back in 1952, for many writers, it all came down to how to get as much money as possible from our resources. To other writers, rapid development and issues of public health are in the forefront. As things have turned out, both of these would be only in the background in a debate on the issues today.

Australia never developed much of a nuclear industry. It does process some of its raw uranium for export, but only to a small degree. It has never yet used uranium to generate electricity, and it never gained access to the (now, not-**so**-elusive) atom bomb secrets.

NEWS ITEMS FROM OVERSEAS

A-bomb troop-test successful. The US army announced on April 21st that one of the largest atom bombs ever made had been exploded in the Nevada desert. On this occasion, 1,500 infantrymen, all volunteers, had crouched in slit trenches about three miles from the point of explosion, and then moved into the blast-region one hour after the blast. The purpose of the test was to determine whether the soldiers would experience any bad effects from the explosion.

The Army, as always, enthused over its published results. Spokesmen said that "the test was an extraordinary success from a military point of view. It lived up to our greatest expectations. It proved to be tremendously important training. The men who were **honoured to be in the front line of an atomic explosion** will have no fear of this new weapon and they will transmit their knowledge in Army camps all over the country."

Thirty five million viewers watched the whole test on TV. They saw that military trucks and vehicles moved into the area almost immediately. Then, an hour later , the infantry moved to join then, and thirty minutes later, paratroops were dropped from planes. In just over two hours, the target area was rendered secure, and this brief war game was declared "over".

Comment. As thousands of servicemen will now attest, these tests carried with them the deadly menace of atomic radiation with its sometimes fatal, sometimes crippling, sometimes hereditary, consequences. The existence of such radiation was evident from Hiroshima and Nagasaki, but from only two such events, it was impossible to draw any scientific conclusions. One of the objectives of **this** test was to look for short term effects, and none were immediately apparent. Longer-term effects were just **now** being studied, through tests such as this.

Build-up continues in Korea. Just a reminder to you that the Reds and the UN negotiators were still messing about, holding meetings, cancelling meetings without explanations, accusing each other of not being sincere, and making accusations of betrayal and duplicity. Meantime, they were both very obviously building up their armed forces in Korea, and appeared to be getting ready for greater hostilities during the summer months. The farce continued as brave and noble men died.

THE COLOUR OF HORSES

It might seem at an initial glance that this is a fairly mundane topic. You might guess that well-bred race horses would know their place and conform to a classification of brown, black, grey and perhaps a few mixes. At second guess, you might add roan, piebald, and spotted, if you know as little as I do. But, I now find out, there is more to it than that. In fact, much more, as the following correspondence indicates.

Letters, G Finlay, Veterinary School, University of Sydney. The first day's sale of thoroughbred yearlings at Randwick showed clearly that, in the classification of the colours of the stock paraded, great confusion exists.

Out of 173 yearlings I inspected in the ring, I found myself unable to agree with the colour classification of 53 of them, or 33 per cent. It is true that many of the cases were examples showing the great difficulty breeders have in distinguishing between bay and brown, and brown and black. Many vendors described the lighter shades of browns as bays. But in one of the best groups offering, ordinary browns were listed as bays.

The grey group showed an unsatisfactory position. One grey was listed as a chestnut. The term "grey" is inadequate. I would prefer an amended classification that would specify that to "grey" should be added the basic colour, so that we would have grey-blacks, grey-browns, grey-bays, and grey-chestnuts. One vendor classified one yearling as "grey or roan." It was a grey chestnut.

The attractive yearling which was referred to as "the spotted wonder" and "another Tetrach" was actually a grey chestnut, and will, of course, become progressively whiter with age.

Comment. Well that appears to have settled that. But, no. It has not. There is a little more to be said.

Letters, H Margie. To judge from Mr G F Finlay's letter on the colour-naming of yearlings, horsemen of today must be sadly lacking in the common knowledge of even a few years ago.

For instance, "black" is very definite. If a horse cannot be described as "black", though it be near black, then it is definitely "dark brown." Where is the difficulty?

Regarding bays, we have (or had) "light" bay, "bright" bay, and "blood" (or dark) bay. The "light" bay was sometimes described as a "yellow" bay, but must have no "golden" tinge in it or it then becomes "chestnut." Here again we have "light", "bright", and "dark" chestnuts.

The colours Mr Finlay would like to have known as "grey chestnut", "grey bay", and "grey brown" are already known to horsemen as "light" roan, "red" roan, and "dark" roan, a fourth being "blue" roan, which is self-explanatory.

Where the white is not evenly mixed with blue, and gives a "patchy" appearance, such marking is called "iron" grey (from the bluish colour of iron or steel). The term "grey black" would be unnecessary. As grey is a mingling of white and black, the word "grey" is sufficient. It may be interesting to note that most "grey" yearlings entered their world as "black" foals, the grey appearing gradually with the growth of the white hairs.

Finally, there is no such thing as a grey chestnut. I repeat that it would be correctly described as "light roan". Let us get back to the old descriptions of colours when writing up catalogues, and I think the difficulties Mr Finlay notes will disappear.

Letters, G Finlay, Veterinary School, University of Sydney. My letter on yearling colours was intended as the first shot in a campaign to ensure greater accuracy in breeding records and pedigrees.

Under the present confusing position, the door is left wide open to mistakes in recording, with ensuing inaccuracies in some pedigrees.

Doping has been practically eliminated through the adoption of scientific tests. It is now time that genetic studies in horse-breeding be carried out and a sound basis of description adopted to protect the authenticity of the stud book records.

For these reasons I deplore the nature of the criticism of my observations of the classification of yearling thoroughbreds by Mr H A Margie, who advocates a return to the old description of colours. He tells us that most greys are born black, and he confuses roan and grey.

All breeders of thoroughbreds in New South Wales who have kept grey stallions know that such sires throw approximately 50 per cent of foals that become grey, and that the great majority of such foals are born brown or bay, a few chestnut, and very rarely indeed a black is born. However, in the Shetland and Percheron breeds, in which black is the predominant basic colour, most greys are born black.

Letters, J King. May I add my quota to the current discussion on the colour-naming of horses?

Mr Margie's definition of roan colourings is better than that of Mr G Finlay, whose introduction of "grey chestnut", grey bay", etc. is both cumbersome and quite unnecessary.

However, I would like to point out that "bay", in which the body-colour can vary from reddish-brown to light chestnut, is distinguished from "chestnut" by always having a black mane and tail.

With "blacks" and "browns", the colour is always decided by the colour of the nose – a horse with a black body and brown nose would be a brown horse.

These classifications are used with English bloodstock.

Letters, H A Margie. Mr G Finlay says I confuse "roan" and "grey", but he himself introduced the element of confusion by earlier taking to task a vendor who had classified a yearling as "grey" or "roan".

Mr Finlay called it a "grey chestnut", and I attempted to show that it would have been correctly classified as a "light roan". Any horseman knows that an animal showing "chestnut" in the coat cannot possibly be in the "grey" class.

Off on the same lines again, Mr Finlay writes regarding the progeny of grey stallions: "50 per cent of them become grey, and most are born bay or brown with a few chestnut. This is quite correct as to colour when born, but such foals do not turn "grey", they become "roan". Only from a black foal will a genuine "grey" evolve.

Letters, Frank Grogan. Most people who have studied horses know that the hairs on a yearling do not change colour. The foal hairs are shed and the grey hairs take their place. No matter how dark brown a horse is, he is not a black.

Grey hairs mixed with chestnut hairs do not produce a red roan. If that were so, then what combination of hairs would produce a blue roan?

The roan is just as definitely a colour as black or bay. In the old days if a bay or chestnut or brown had grey hairs, it was alluded to as flecked with grey hairs.

Neither Mr Finlay nor Mr Margie mentions a very common but none the less beautiful marking, namely, the dapples.

As a boy of nine I began cutting up dead horses to find out how they were made, and what made the machinery of the horse work. Many years of this type of study proved to me that many of the ideas held by people concerning horses, and what enables them to move themselves, are absolutely wrong, and provide very strong argument why Mr Finlay should secure the cooperation he invites.

Comment. Mr Grogan was apparently a man of many parts. Mainly horses'.

ANZACS IN THE NEWS

When ANZAC Day came round, 8,000 hardy souls greeted it with a dawn service in Sydney. After that, at 9am, 14,000 war veterans started moving off from marshalling yards to march towards the Cenotaph in Martin Place. There was a light drizzle at the time, but over the next hour, the rain got heavier, so that by 10am officials of the RSL decided that the march had to be cancelled. The servicemen were dispersed, and the 100,000 spectators went home to dry out. This was the first time ever that Sydney's ANZAC march had been cancelled.

That did not stop the revelry among the ex-Diggers. They all met up in their pre-organised watering holes, and made the most of their day. Pub closing hours were unofficially relaxed by a few hours in many locations, so that by closing time, many of them were completely sozzled. All this gay abandon, as the newspapers made plain over the next few days, had its consequences.

First, they reported that 400 people had been treated in hospitals for injuries over the course of the day and night. This was in Sydney city alone, and it is reasonable to think that across the nation the toll must have been in the thousands. You can add to that the thousands who did not report to hospitals.

Second, they printed dozens of Letters that talked about how the Diggers were justified in their antics on this day.

Letters, R Hemming, C of E. I am writing in deep sorrow and distress at the prostitution of Anzac Day into a drunken revel.

In order to prevent a repetition of the disgraceful scenes that marred the ending of this Anzac Day, I strongly suggest that the sale and consumption of alcoholic beverages be totally banned on Anzac Day. If this be not possible, then I am of the opinion that **April 25 should not be a public holiday.**

I deeply regret that any citizen should feel compelled to make such suggestions regarding the observance of a day held sacred to the memory of those who died for us. But the situation that has developed in the Anzac Days of the past ten years or so leaves no option.

With some members of my Young People's Fellowship, I was on Strathfield railway station in the evening of Anzac Day. Two drunken men wearing the ribbons of ex-Servicemen persisted in attempting to maul some of the girls in the party under my charge. Only the most blatant verbal persuasions, backed up by the obvious but unuttered threat of physical force by myself and the young men of my party, induced them to desist. Amongst those on that station, there were about 12 ex-Servicemen and Servicemen in uniform in various stages of drunkenness.

My assistant in the work of the fellowship, a married woman of high repute in this district, was grossly insulted when by her manner she made known her disgust at this unseemliness.

Drunken men were on the train between Strathfield and Parramatta, and we had to exercise the utmost vigilance to protect our girls from the possibility of further insult.

If future Anzac Days are to be as they were on Friday, then I shall certainly keep my family and any others in my charge on that day as far away from Anzac celebrations as I can. Failing some drastic alteration in the manner of observing Anzac Days in the future I would earnestly counsel any young woman to keep out of Sydney on that day unless accompanied by a hefty male escort.

I do not blame the men concerned so much as an attitude towards Anzac Day which demands its commemoration in a veritable flood of drink.

Letters, E J Gaffey, Waverley Methodist Mission. Is it possible to reverence the memory of a brave man with a bottle of grog? Undoubtedly it is not, and I feel sure that the immortal would not sanction such sacrilege of the fallen.

Anzac Day, 1952, with its official tolerance of crime and disorder, is an example of the depths to which humanity sank during the past wars.

Letters, William Yeo, State President, RSL, Australia. Until noon the day is dedicated to commemorate the sacrifice of our departed comrades – the men who gave their lives to ensure the right of Mr Hemming and others to criticise the doings of other people. They died so that those girls in Mr Hemming's charge would not be subjected to the fate of most women who fell into the clutches of the Japanese soldiery.

Conservatively, 75,000 ex-Servicemen set out after noon to celebrate all that the original Anzac Day, and the many glorious feats of our men at arms since, means – still in accordance with the accepted policy of the RSL applicable to the afternoon of Anzac Day.

Out of that 75,000 apparently a few hundred "got drunk". I do not ask Mr Hemming's interpretation of "drunk" but from the tone of his letter one can guess that what was probably an overdone bit of horse-play was regarded as a serious threat.

Thousands of Diggers celebrating Anzac Day afternoon in our accepted tradition had daughters and womenfolk of their own in Sydney that day cheering their fathers, brothers, and their comrades and thanking God that these men had interposed their bodies as a barrier between them and a bestial enemy.

Letters, M N O'Reilly. Each year as Anzac Day approaches, statements appear in which the RSL (and similar ex-Servicemen's organisations) lay emphasis on the importance of an adequate flow of intoxicating liquors in order that the day may be fittingly observed. Spokesmen for the ULVA and the breweries then give solemn assurance that everything possible will be done to see that beer is laid on.

Surely in remembering fallen comrades it is not necessary to spend half of the one day set apart each year for that purpose in drunken orgies and brawling, larrikin street scenes.

Letters, Dorothy Gellie. As an ex-Army Sister I cannot sit quietly by while the ex-Servicemen are condemned.

My memories of these men during the war – particularly in New Guinea between 1942 and 1944 and in other war zones – compel me to defend them. Surely there is sufficient tolerance and understanding to soften if not obliterate the criticism that continually crops up. After all, it is only one day in a year, and it was every day in quite a few years for the men who fought for us.

When war clouds are not imminent and one is comfortably settled, I suppose it is easy to be righteous and critical.

Letters, J Golder. In my opinion, the Anzac Day disturbances were brought about in order to discredit the Anzacs and Anzac Day by a certain element living amongst us who are definitely anti-British.

Letters, R Hemming, St Paul's Church of England, Wentworthville. Do not Mr Yeo and the RSL realise that their advocacy of a "wet" Anzac afternoon will wash it into the limbo of forgotten things? Nowadays it is hard enough for those of us who endeavour to mould the minds of the young to inculcate respect for things that matter. How much more difficult when those who should be leading in the respect for Anzac are advocating its degradation in drink?

The attitude of the police in "turning the blind eye" to things they are paid to prevent is unlawful. I strongly suggest to the Commissioner of Police that the situation in Sydney on Anzac Day was such as to cause him to cancel this misguided leniency.

Letters, Maurice Lloyd. In reply to Rev R W Hemming: It was my privilege to be a soldier in the 6th Division. After the Anzac Day march, "our mob" held a reunion. Our ex-commanding officer spoke a short, sharp speech.

He said: "Gentlemen, in the morning we remember our fallen comrades; in the afternoon, we celebrate with the living." That man's brother was killed in Crete. He shared his last smoke with his batman during the escape from Greece. My father died at Gallipoli.

I had a few over the eight on the 25th of last month. Do you blame me?

CLERGY'S ATTITUDE TO GROG

The above Letters from Messrs Hemming and Gaffey left no doubt about how they felt about drinking grog to excess. It is fair to say that many clergy would have agreed with them and, further, a sizeable number would have liked to ban grog at all times. On the other hand, a fair majority would have been happy to see alcohol consumed in moderation, under the decent conditions that Australian hotels and brewers seemed determined not to provide.

The two views on this matter shown below are by no means typical, but they do come from a numerically substantial part of our society that would have **welcomed total abstinence**.

News item, April 10. Parishioners of St Paul's Church of England in Canberra were warned today that they would not be married in the Church if they were in any way intoxicated. The Rev Ross Border stated that "if either bride or groom arrives at the Church in even a slightly intoxicated state, I shall not marry them. Further, any guest who arrives intoxicated will be asked to leave, and the marriage will not proceed until he or she has left." He added that to make a wedding an excuse for getting drunk is warranted neither socially nor morally.

News item, April 30. The Reverend Charles Tomlinson, President of the NSW Temperance Society, said yesterday that **the extension of hotel hours** would expose the community to **greater** moral harm than did existing pig-swill conditions in hotels today. He of course wanted all hotels permanently closed, but if there were to be hotels, he did not want to see them open after 6pm.

"Later trading hours would enlist more immoderate drinkers and introduce more women to drinking. Great moral harm will come from later drinking. The cure of the problem rests on faith in God through Christ. Only as people are built up in Christian character can we overcome the drink evil."

NEWS AND VIEWS

Letters, J Lascelles. I read with surprise the suggestion of the Primate of Australia, Dr Mowill, that we should **rename Australian aborigines "Black Australians"** to help free them from a feeling of inferiority.

Does Dr. Mowll really think that this will help in the problem of the Aboriginal? I suggest that the name would immediately bring fresh complexes and inhibitions to those who were originally the owners of our country.

It would be a better idea to call Aborigines "Australians," and all the white population – whether New Australians or Old Australians – "White Australians."

Why "Aborigines" should need replacing is beyond me. I imagine that any "original Australian" would prefer to be called an "abo" than a "Black Australian."

AMATEUR HOURS

These competitions were about to become popular on radio. Half a dozen networks round Australia ran these programs at various times over the next decade, and they were very successful The essence was that a handful of persons each week would perform some audible act, and be judged by the studio audience or the wider listening public. The winner would get a prize, and in most cases, go on to the finals a few weeks later.

Many competitors were singers, or violinists or pianists. There were a fair number who practiced the now-dead skill of whistling, others could yodel till the cows came home, and the occasional gum-leaf player squeaked his way through *Click go the Shears* and *Waltzing Matilda*.

Bob Dyer and Jack Davey at various times took a turn at being compare. Colgate Palmolive was a persistent sponsor.

MAY: HAPPENINGS IN KOREA

The hopeless dithering in Korea continued on as usual. Neither the Russian-Chinese nor the American-UN parties to the conflict were in a hurry to end hostilities, so that **so-called armistice negotiations dragged on and on**. On the battlefield, the opposing armies were moving their lines back and forth at regular intervals without any major battles. In the air, the combats were a lot fiercer, but given that both sides had an inexhaustible supply of aircraft, it mattered little whether one side or other lost ten or maybe twenty planes in a day.

In the month of May however, incidents occurred that drove home the folly of this whole situation. The UN had by now captured about 100,000 prisoners who they held in various locations camps round the area. One group of these, about 70,000 in number, were on the off-shore island of Koje, in a number of camps. A few months earlier four of these men had been killed, and this had prompted the prisoners into a unified body of resistors more than normally opposed to their captors.

US Brigadier General Dodd was commandant of the camps on the island. On May 14, he visited one such camp with only a small detachment of guards, and was taken prisoner by the inmates. He was held for almost a day, and was persuaded to create and sign a document that expressed remorse for American exploits in the war and in the camp. He signed a statement that promised "an immediate end to the insulting behavior and abuse by American troops, and an end to torture, forcible threatening, confinement, mass murdering, gun and machine-gunning, germ warfare, and experiments with A-Bombs." He also promised to cease the forceful interrogation of prisoners.

Another General, Colson, had been appointed to replace Dodd. He replied to the prisoners, with "I do admit that in the past there have been many instances of bloodshed where many prisoners have been killed and wounded by UN troops. I can assure you that in the future P-O-Ws can expect humane treatment. I will do all in my power to eliminate further violence and bloodshed." **Dodd was then released** and he returned to the US lines.

The US General Clark, head of the Korean operation overall, then – **as you might expect** – issued statements **saying that the admissions above had been obtained by duress, and therefore were forcefully repudiated.** Indeed he was right in this, but still, in a war that was being conducted under the microscope of world public opinion, the whole debacle was an unwelcome episode for the US. Opponents of the war asked hard questions. How come our security is so bad that a top ranking military officer can be captured by unarmed prisoners? In one of our own camps? Were the alleged atrocities true?. Was poison gas being used? Were prisoners being killed? **Within the US**, such questions were brazened out, with much breast-beating. **But elsewhere in the world**, much of the mud stuck, especially for those who wanted it to stick. The incident became a memorable propaganda setback that was not forgotten readily.

Comment. As a footnote I add that on May 31, US troops killed four more prisoners on Koje, and wounded 14 others. The Oz Press all said that the shootings were in self defence, and there is no reason to argue with that. But I add, for what it is worth, that it must have been obvious that such incidents would keep recurring, both here and at other camps, and that both sides should each repatriate their 100,000 prisoners without delay, and stop the futile point-scoring that was keeping them in prison.

Second Comment. The events on Koje were well reported in the Press for over two weeks. There was also a great deal of Editorial comment on the subject. But not once did the news report ever get off Page Three of the newspapers. And not one **Letter** was published by the major Dailies. This war was labeled then, and since, as **the "forgotten war" and public interest in it lessened as it dragged on.**

LET'S ACCEPT OUR FATE AND SMILE

Letter writers were prolific, and very ready to tell everyone else what to do, and how to act. Below is a Letter from a firm Liberal Party supporter who thinks that acceptance of our fate is a blessing for the nation.

Letters, Lyle H Moore, NSW President of the Liberal Party. During World Wars I and II the Australian political parties and Governments largely sank their differences. The forces of labour and management modified their disputations and pooled their efforts, and the people who suffered inconvenience or hardship through economic restraints, for the most part bore them uncomplainingly.

That was patriotism at work. But what a different picture there is today, when the nation is waging a "cold" war against world Communism's threat that is getting more cold each month!

Irresponsibility is demonstrated daily by **the Labour Party** in its opposition to the Federal Government measures to get Australia ready to defend herself against a Communist foe, and at the same time to cure the economic ills from which, in common with most other countries, we are suffering.

Self-interest is very understandably being shown by those who are experiencing temporary economic setbacks as a result of these measures. Such persons could give valuable national assistance if they **were cheerfully to accept their present burdens** in the knowledge that the steps taken are designed for their ultimate advantage.

Is it too much today to ask all people, all groups for selflessness, responsibility of approach, appreciation of the day's serious problems, abandonment of political manoeuvring, and a sincere national outlook on these grave national matters – **in short, for patriotism**?

They must remember that, when they cannot understand the reason for some Commonwealth measure, they have not the broad national information canvas before them that has been viewed by Federal Cabinet. Unavoidably, they are **looking on Australia from a very small personal** or Labor Party window which can only give them an incomplete picture.

No Government, in its right mind, does unpopular things if there are effective alternatives. The fact that the Government has had to take unpalatable steps, therefore, speaks for its courage and its devotion to Australia's welfare.

If the Government had this courage, and this devotion, surely the Labor Party, the self-interested, and the indifferent, can respond by facing up to the present grave situation with equal courage and devotion! That would be patriotism in practice!

Comment. Obviously this Letter, from the President of the NSW **Liberal Party**, was supportive of the various policies that the current **Liberal** Federal Government had introduced. But the wider question raised by the Letter is should we as citizens always cheerfully accept with good spirit and understanding **every move that the Government makes**? And if we did, **is this patriotism**? I can think of a few people who would have a bit to say on both these questions.

THE FORTY HOUR WEEK

A few industries had by now gained a 40-hour working week. Most unionised workers still worked 44 hours and a few toiled for 48. Most professionals and tradesmen had no legal limit. Butin unionised circles, the topic was right on the agenda..

Letters, M Rathbone. Those who advocate and those who oppose the 40-hour week are voluble in their opinions, but rarely does one hear anybody weighing up **the pros and cons** of the situation.

It would appear that the 40-hour week allows more rest and recreation to the worker, and it often enables the more ambitious types to take on two separate jobs under different masters. It automatically raises wages by giving less labour for the same money. It enables many people to undertake work on their own account around their homes, and most certainly makes a little more daylight available for these pastimes.

On the other hand, the 40-hour week upsets many a good man's working equilibrium. He finds he cannot get self-gratification out of his work, and often goes home to several hours of utter boredom, both before and after his evening meal. He finds he has to **wait longer for the local picture show to open** and, this being so, he gets to bed no earlier on many occasions. He has too much time to brood, and in cases where he takes on another job to kill the ennui, he works more than he should, and then gets unfit to do any job properly.

These features of a worker's life hang on the fine thread of a mere four hours' work which is not being done today. If we spent those extra four hours at our jobs, we would be more in a line with the rest of the world, more contented with our jobs, prouder of our independence, and more gratified at the end of the day.

Comment. The 40-hour week had been introduced to Oz only in the last two years, across the Commonwealth and various State work forces. Here we have a writer who is not convinced of its worth, and implies the extra leisure is not to our benefit. On balance, though, I am not too borne down by the consequences, so I would be quite happy if we stick to 40 hours.

OUR POLITICAL PARTIES

Letters, Employer. Many people must surely view with concern the growing bitterness of the conflict between the two political parties. In the personal abuse, the hatreds, and the struggle for power, the welfare of Australia is likely to be forgotten.

The parties appear to differ on every conceivable point and contest every Act of Legislation brought forward by the opposing party, yet rarely alter it when they get into power. Employers generally fear that this radical difference of opinion and lack of tolerance will lead to further industrial unrest, class hatred and reprisals.

It should be remembered that although the shortage of labour is not now so bad, there is still a considerable shortage of skilled labour, and this position may continue for many years. Common-sense, therefore, tells us that only by cooperation, goodwill and the very best use of the labour available, can we hope to produce anything like the goods and services required by the community at a reasonable cost.

Is it not time our politicians acted as reasonable people, ceased abusing one another, and got on with the wise government of the country?

Comment.   No, my friendly readers. This Letter was **not** written some time this year, say 2016. It was in fact from May 26, 1952. A lot of things have changed since then, but some things are still exactly the same.

RECRUITING FOR THE ARMY

Letters, H Robertson, (Lieut.-General), Director of Recruiting, Victoria Barracks, Melbourne. There are still at least 500,000 young men between the ages of 19 and 26 in Australia who have not served in the military and appear to show no inclination to do so.

Is there any reason why an Australian should not qualify for full citizenship by preparing himself to defend his land, his home, his loved ones, and his way of life? After all, if this country is worth fighting for, and if we are forced to fight for it, let us have some commonsense and teach ourselves how to fight.

Your correspondent who signed himself "Young Australian" suggests that apprentices, university and technical college students, doctors, dentists, carpenters, engineers, plumbers, and lawyers should not be required to train themselves to aid in the defence of their country. This is a strange theory, because men from every one of those callings and professions are needed to make the modern war machine work efficiently – in fact many of the most notable men in those callings and professions have given very distinguished service to Australia in the Armed Services.

There cannot be, **and will not be**, any excuse for men in those callings to avoid their national responsibility to play their part in the defence of their country.

Comment. Director of **Recruiting**, Robertson, was looking at things from the point of view of **his job**. It was a difficult job, because at the time there was no credible military threat to Australia from any direction. The interesting thing to me about this Letter is that Robertson was still using the rhetoric and sentiments of WWII to stir up patriots, seven years after the War had finished. By now most people, though still conscious of the terrible years not so long ago, just wanted to put it at the back of their mind, and get on with life. The fervour of Robertson's Letter seemed strangely out of place in this care-free time for the nation.

CAR COLLISIONS

The number of cars on the road was a lot less than in later years. Still, collisions were occurring at an alarming rate. I enclose two Letters that show current thinking on causes and remedies.

Letters, W Lawrence, Superintendent of Traffic, Sydney. I read with interest the letter from Dr MacIntosh. I respect his medical knowledge, but suggest that his view of the "four major factors which stand out as obvious causes of motor accidents" is a little out of focus.

Figures do not lie. Records at the Traffic Office show that the two major causes of road collisions are **speed and drunken driving.** Not exercising proper care at intersections, and failure to give way to the vehicle on the right are the next two major causes.

The doctor says that "speed is rarely a cause of accidents if a vehicle is in competent hands". Surely this is a sweeping statement. Competent drivers are very rarely involved in collision through speed or through any other cause, and, furthermore, really competent drivers seldom speed.

Let us view this tragic problem of the toll of the road in its true light. It is purely an unnecessary evil. It is brought about by reckless, thoughtless, inconsiderate drivers, riders, and pedestrians.

The police do not "watch only for speed" on the roads, as the doctor suggests. All types of traffic breaches are detected amongst all types of vehicles in all types of places. The number of traffic breaches detected in New South Wales averages 7,050 a week. Breaches for speed make up only a percentage of this total, and breaches against pedestrians are not included.

More strict tests and education for drivers may be of some value, but lack of knowledge is not killing our road users – it is failure to put that knowledge into practice which brings tragedy.

Letters, L Howell. My own experience includes light and heavy trucks, cars, motor cycles, and push cycles. I support strongly the doctor's views.

It is, as he says, the lack of competent hands on the wheel, and the lack of anticipatory thought in the driver that are the main contributing factors in accidents.

Adults and adolescents do not take kindly to regimentation and education. These are both badly needed to inculcate a practical appreciation and understanding of both road courtesy and driving technique.

Comment. On first reading, it might seem that some things do not change. However, some measures that have been introduced have made a big difference. For examples, drink-driving laws, seat belts, and expressways. They have reduced the toll quite a lot.

AUSTRALIAN WHALERS READY TO SAIL

Press release, Mat 1952. The Australian whaling season will open tomorrow when slim, high-bowed chaser-vessels put to sea from **the Western Australian coast. East coast whaling** will begin on a large scale next Saturday for the first time since the days of Ben Boyd in the last century. Four Australian companies expect to take 1,750 whales (worth about 1,500,000 Pounds) from western and eastern waters before the season ends in October.

There are two large groups of humpback whales (the type most commonly caught off Australia) in the Antarctic – one group south of the Indian Ocean and another south of New Zealand. Each April, these monsters swim north to mate and breed in the warmer waters of the sub-tropical zone. One group swims past the Western Australian coast and the other passes New Zealand and Australia's eastern coast.

The Press tell us that humpback whales, each weighing between 35 and 40 tons, yield about eight tons of oil as well as many valuable by-products. Although the price has fallen recently, oil is still worth about 80 Pounds sterling a ton. Australia's tanning, textile, and rope industries are users, but the biggest demand comes from **the margarine industries** abroad. Whale oil is also used in the manufacture of paints, candles, cosmetics, soap, and glycerine.

The Federal Government each year places a ceiling on the number of whales which may be caught in coastal waters. This season's quota has been raised from 1,200 to 1,750. Western Australian whalers will take 1,250 whales.

A new Australian company, Whale Products, has a permit to take 500 whales from Australia's eastern waters this year.

There has been no large-scale whaling on this coast since 1860. Ben Boyd established Boyd Town on Twofold Bay, and for many years operated a bay and deep-sea whaling fleet. By 1860, Australian waters had been almost worked out by the indiscriminate slaughter which had gone on for more than 50 years.

At Whale Industries, last November, there were only two army buildings on the factory site at Tangalooma in Queensland. Now, there exists a slipway of heavy logs and a cleansing deck of reinforced concrete on which workers can handle four whales at once. Also two huge cookers in which crude whale oil is extracted from blubber and bone, pumping equipment and tanks to provide 200 gallons of water a minute. The factory is now ready to handle and process nine whales an hour.

Whaling, although the season is short, is one of the best-paid occupations in Australia today. The lowest paid man in the industry last season was the hygiene officer, who sprayed flies. He received 30 Pounds a week. At the other end of the scale, a top gunner on a chaser earned more than 4,000 Pounds a season with bonuses.

Comment. This industry has now gone, and would not be too popular if it wanted to make a comeback.

NEWS AND TRIVIA

Letters, J Lewis. Annual factory, pastoral, and agricultural return forms will soon be distributed **by the police** for the State Government Statistician.

The forms are delivered by two police officers, one generally a sergeant, travelling by motor car or **cycle with side-car**. Why cannot these forms be dispatched through the post, thus saving valuable petrol and the time of police officers?

Letters, L Anderson. In order to foster more interest in meat quality, the Royal Agricultural Society is reported to have arranged a miniature school at the Homebush Abattoirs. Members of the public are to be taken free of charge to the abattoirs.

Might I suggest that if better quality meat is to be obtained, what is needed is not schools for the public at Homebush, but the killing of fat stock painlessly and as near as possible to the pastures where they were fattened.

It has always been recognised that country-killed meat is of much finer quality than from animals which have been trucked long distances, bruised, starved, and knocked about before being slaughtered. Is it any wonder that meat from these animals is often wretched quality? On top of all this the loss of weight, through wastage and shrinkage, is colossal.

All stock slaughtered at abattoirs should be immediately rendered unconscious either by shooting or by the use of the **Captive Bolt pistol**. As early as 1893 the Government of Switzerland passed an Act forbidding butchers to kill without previous stunning; Germany, Denmark, Italy, Holland, and Scandinavia quickly followed.

The use of the Captive Bolt pistol has been made compulsory in all abattoirs in Victoria. If this were done in New South Wales, and if more stock were slaughtered in the country, there would be far more meat available and of very much better quality.

JUNE: MORE ON KOREA AND KOJE

I do not want to harp back to the Korean fiasco all the time, but events in Koje in early June leave me no choice. As the month of June progressed, things there really hotted up. It all started when the Allies discovered that the various prison compounds restraining the prisoners were connected by a large series of tunnels that also extended to places outside the prisons. This meant that agitators were free to move round at will organising resistance, and that military materials could be smuggled in as they chose. The scene was being set for a large-scale break-out that was clearly being planned.

Over the next few days, Allied troops moved at their risk into the compounds, and tried to destroy the tunnels. But there were so many of them that their efforts were of little use. After that, aggravations occurred daily, with a few prisoners killed and wounded every day. Finally, the US let it be known that the compounds would be reduced in size and relocated, to dilute the very real power of the truculent prisoners. From June 9th, it was obvious that certain compounds intended to resist this move and, for example, the blacksmiths facilities among the prisoners were working day and night to make spears, weapons, and projectiles for the looming show-down.

At 6am on June 11th, US tanks and 750 troops began to move into Compound 76, housing 6,000 prisoners. They were led by tanks and flanked by armoured cars. Their aim was to force the occupants to assemble into groups of 150 and march into much smaller compounds prepared nearby. The US flame-throwers were blazing, and they hurled barrages of tear-gas and concussion grenades before them. They met stiff resistance from the unarmed prisoners who had retreated to the slit-trenches they had built in the last week. Tents and wooden buildings burst into flames when grenades started fires and set off gasoline in secret caches of petrol. "We fought them with bayonets, and we fought them with fists", said US soldiers.

In two and a half hours, all resistance was stifled and the prisoners filed out. Other Compounds had watched and learned, and there was no resistance from them. A total of 106 prisoners were killed and 400 were wounded. One US soldier was killed.

Comment. It is not for me to judge how necessary this action was. It seems that some drastic action was needed to prevent a serious attack on the US military forces on the island. Whether this particular approach was the right one or not, no one will ever be able to judge. Yet, given this was a war being fought for propaganda purposes, it certainly was a setback for American interests. Of course, in nations like the US and Britain and Oz, criticism of the US was muted as usual, but in much of the world, it was flagrant. The situation, **as presented there,** was that with no provocation, the US sent its army into the perfectly peaceful compounds and shot up and killed hundreds (or thousands) of unarmed, sleeping, starving prisoners. When people want to believe this type of propaganda, no argument in the world will prevail against it.

Second comment. For a single day, the day of the attack on the Compound, news from Korea found the front page of the Oz Press. And for the first time in months, a Letter-writer had something to say. His Letter gave a rousing hurrah for the war, and reassured people that we were the goodies, and that the war was indeed serving some useful purpose.

Letters, Davis Hughes, MLA. The long-drawn-out truce talks in Korea and the emphasis given to the activities of the USA contingent in the United Nations' forces have caused Australians to forget that for two years Australian forces have been engaged in front-line action under harsh conditions as a vital part of the British Commonwealth forces.

Occasionally, the calm surface of our apathy is faintly stirred by such incidents as a revolt on Koje Island, an attack on Communist power installations or a remembrance that this week marks the second anniversary of the campaign, but then the ripples subside and all is peace once more.

The whole Australian nation should realise that our own men are fighting daily a battle against Communist aggression. Each week our men are being killed, each week our men are being committed to Communist POW camps, each week Australian homes are being shattered by the news of husbands and sons dying for a cause, **the successful outcome of which is vital to our security and freedom**.

The nation needs to be awakened to this position and I believe we should focus full attention on Korea and the efforts of our men there, fighting shoulder to shoulder, wing-tip to wing-tip, with soldiers, sailors, and airmen from New Zealand, Canada, and Great Britain.

I believe we should have an Australian-wide "Korea Day" of prayer, thanksgiving, and remembrance, and combine with it a concerted effort, to show our awareness of the courage, fortitude, and gallantry of our men, by providing from the people of Australia a practical token of our very real appreciation of the sacrifices being made by fellow-Australians.

I would urge most strongly that a nation-wide move be made to stir the Australian public conscience into a deep awareness of the significance of Korea and the importance of the participation of our own men in it. The Churches and Press could give a very real lead to the nation by calling to the people of the Commonwealth to observe a national "Korea Day."

Comment. Mr Hughes's earnest plea fell on ears that continued to be deaf, and the war continued to be forgotten.

NO SHORTAGE OF BOARDS

By the time the War ended in 1945, our governments had all sorts of **controls** over most of our activities and over most things we ate and drank and purchased. By 1950, many of these restrictions had been removed. For example, rationing of butter, clothing and petrol had all gone. But other means of control lingered, for all sorts or reasons. Thus, there was a multitude of Government Boards, both State and Federal, that kept their tight little hands on certain activities, and imposed regulations on citizens. The existence of these Boards was very much resented by the population, but getting rid of them proved difficult.

One such Board was the Rice Board, which regulated the flow of rice in Australia. This was then a nation with a liking for rice **as a Sunday pudding**, and was just coming to like it with our curried prawns from the Chinesie on Friday nights. But it was not widely used in most Anglo homes. On the other hand, our small Asian population during the War had established that it was essential for their well-being and so, with limited supplies available at that time, had been granted their rations for the period. This meant that rice went off the menu for Oz homes during the War, and for a few years after that.

By 1952, however, our production was quite adequate to meet our needs and to feed our own Asian residents. In fact it had grown to the stage where we could export quite a quantity to Britain. Enter now the Rice Board which had control over distribution of all our rice.

The rice crop was badly damaged in 1952. Given the small quantity, the Board decided that local Asians should be fed, and after that the remainder should go to **meet contracts they had made with Britain.** That meant that there was none for home consumption. This nation had no extra money to import rice from anywhere else, so non-Asian Oz housewives missed out completely for the year.

Many Oz locals were peeved, and this Letter below is typical.

Letters, Mary Mayberry. I was all for Bundles for Britain during the War. I sent as many as anyone. For five years after the War, I was happy to support Britain by giving up meat, butter, clothing, petrol and tobacco so that the British could get more of these things. But by the time 1950 came, to ask me to continue this sacrifice was too much. **Then** I thought it was time we as a nation looked after ourselves and Britain did the same for itself.

Now I find that we have a poor rice crop, and that Britain and its Empire will get **our** quota for this year. We have, it appears, a Board that says this must happen because "we are contracted to make such deliveries." They say this as though it is an excuse for themselves.

What they should be saying is that they entered into contracts overseas with operators who were smarter than they were, and that they are not capable of backing out of the contract.

Have they not heard of Force Majeure which the British use every time they renege on delivery? Have they not heard of "unfortunate delays to delivery beyond our control" and other ruses that the overseas traders pull on Australia all the time? Have they realised that with contracts written for the next five years, we could be without rice for that period?

When will we be rid of these hopeless and inefficient Boards?

BURL IVES IN OZ

The American folk-singer, Burl Ives, arrived in Australia in middle-June. Ives was a well known singer of popular folk-songs with a voice which, according to US music critic John Rockwell, "had the sheen and finesse of opera without its latter-day vulgarities, and without the pretentions of operatic ritual. It was genteel in expressive impact without being genteel in social conformity. And it moved people."

Ives had many fans in this country, and was famous for songs such as *Blue Tail Fly* and *Lavender Blue*. He was in trouble on a number of occasions with churches in America for his singing of *Foggy Foggy Dew*. This song contained the lyrics:

"So I put her into bed, and I covered up her head,

Just to keep her from the foggy foggy dew"

Then it went on to say:

"Now I am a bachelor and I live with my son....

And every time I look into his eyes he reminds me of the fair young maid."

In 1952, in the make-believe puritanical world of Hollywood and parts of show-business America, this was regarded as a suggestion that hanky-panky had occurred, and so there should be no mention of it. Still, Ives was able to thrive on publicity such as this, and he went on to make many successful films and TV series.

In Oz, his concerts were all sell-outs, and he was a huge success. Though one gentleman raised a matter that cast just a tiny shadow on his visit. It concerned a concert given by him at Newcastle, with the hallowed ABC orchestra.

News Item, Newcastle. The Principal of the Newcastle Conservatorium of Music, Mr H Lobb, said tonight that he would protest to the ABC for including the folk-singer Burl Ives in their subscription concert. Mr Lobb said tonight: "The ABC, when they encourage the public to buy tickets for subscription concerts, indicate that they will hear good and important music. Burl Ives's singing does not come under that heading. I intend to make a protest to the ABC for including Ives as one of their artists in the subscription concert series.

"I agree that he may be a great artist in his own sphere; but so is Harpo Marx and Frank Sinatra. Ives is not a serious artist and he does not present serious music.

"I have often heard of discrimination against Newcastle in the music world. The ABC's action seems to bear this out.

"In Sydney the people that attended Ives's concerts were not the same as those that went to hear orchestral music at subscription concerts."

Comment. There was no evidence that Ives lost much weight worrying about this niggle.

TOUGH TIMES FOR WORKERS?

The nation's economy kept going slowly backwards, and this emboldened various employer groups to start various campaigns to reduce workers' conditions.

Letters, Kingsley Laffer. It is very much to be hoped that the three employers' organisations concerned can be persuaded to withdraw their applications to the Arbitration Court **for wage-reduction.**

The expectation aroused that wages, and therefore prices, may fall, is likely to induce manufacturers to postpone investment in plant, retailers to keep stock replacement orders to a minimum, and consumers to hold off buying. Serious unemployment and business depression could easily result. Industrial relations might be worsened for many years ahead.

The benefit to business of eventual wage-reduction is extremely problematical. Costs would certainly be reduced, but so also would the amount people have to spend; business in general would be no better off, though businesses with a high proportion of labour costs might gain at the expense of those with low labour costs. No ultimate benefit that can be envisaged is likely to offset the probable severe effect now of the wage-reduction applications.

Comment. As it turned out wages were not reduced, though increases granted by the various Courts in the months ahead were not as generous as they might have been. At the time, though, pushes for wage reductions were very real and worrying to workers.

Other writers spoke up.

Letters, Paul Pickle. The continual cry, "We will never return to the 44-hour week," is to me exasperating, nauseating, and thoroughly defeatist.

The introduction of the 40-hour week has been followed by economic and business chaos, disruption, anxiety, frustration, and a colossal waste of time and increased cost of living.

It has had an extremely fair trial, though from the outset it was doomed to failure because of the utter stupidity of the premises upon which it was based. A week of 44 hours will hurt no one – in fact, **it will keep them in good health and out of mischief.**

The ones who are most strongly opposed to a return to previous conditions are probably working 50 or 60 hours a week – with this vast difference, that they are being paid considerable overtime on the extra hours worked, notwithstanding that one of the inducements put forward by the protagonists of the 40 hours was that it would provide rest and relaxation. What blatant hypocrisy!

Letters, David Walker.   It is distressing to find a correspondent resorting to contemptuous abuse of the working public with an accusation of hypocrisy and using vague generalisations about the economic situation unsupported by all relevant facts and figures – this in a time when clear sober thought is needed.

Need I mention that the impertinent assertion that a 44-hour week will keep "them out of mischief" is more suited for schoolmasters' jargon than for a responsible citizen to employ in a public controversy.

Those men working "a probable 50 to 60 hours weekly" often do so, myself included, in order to pay for the erection, by themselves at week-ends and with family , of their own homes.

We, at least, have no time to be "thoroughly exasperated and nauseated," and the charge of being defeatist collapses when faced with the fact of our achievement of homes self-built, in addition to working a regular 40 hours plus 10 to 20 hours overtime. We have also, we hope, preserved our good manners.

Comment. After a long fight, for years, the 40-hour week finally was gaining acceptance as an on-going standard. Though challenges kept coming for decades.

TRIVIA: TWO INTERESTING LETTERS

Letters, R Chisholm, ex-RAF, Bombay. It has upset me to learn from the *Herald* of May 13 that the Australian Director-General of Civil Aviation described the flight from England to Australia by Martin and Mirtle Cherry as a "suicide flight".

[Captain and Mrs Cherry left Koepang (Timor) for Darwin on May 11 in a single-engine Proctor aircraft, and did not reach their destination.]

The Cherrys cannot answer this charge themselves, so I am writing in their defence. My wife and I flew a single-engined Auster from England to India and for most of the route we flew with the Cherrys.

Apart from the fact that we became personally very fond of this charming couple, I gained the greatest respect for Martin Cherry as a pilot. Under his camouflage of the happy-go-lucky dare-devil, he was a sane and cautious pilot who knew the route well.

As to the charge that a flight in a single-engine aircraft on this route is suicide, the answer is that aviation insurance companies will insure such flights at quite reasonable premiums and these insurance companies do not insure "suicide flights".

As far as I know, the Cherrys carried no dinghy, food, or water, and their guns were taken from them by the Indian Customs at Ahmedabad. This information would have been on the flight-clearance form at Koepang if the aerodrome officials had done their job properly. It is clear that there was no point in searching the sea for more than 24 hours at most.

On the subject of the cost of the search, I would like to request search organisations to cease issuing sensational cost figures for these searches. A large proportion of the cost would anyway be incurred in normal training and should not be set against any particular incident.

As to this particular search, I will give you the answer that Martin Cherry would have given: if it costs too much, then don't look for him. The Cherrys would have made the trip whether or not there had been a search organisation.

Those who grudge the cost of the search may like to know that when my wife and I were overdue at Cyprus, Martin Cherry was standing by with his single-engine aircraft to search 300 miles of sea at his own expense when the message came in that we had landed safely at Beirut. He was not a rich man and we were almost strangers to him at that time.

Surely Australia owes her discovery and development to people like the Cherrys. Surely there is still a place there for those with this spirit.

Letters, Pedagogue.   There is, I believe, a move on the part of women teachers of the non-governmental schools to form a union so as to demand an increase in salaries.

I grant that 95 per cent of these teachers **are working for salaries well below the basic wage**, but it seems a great pity that the one section of the community which has hitherto given a thoroughly unselfish and truly vocational service to their fellow citizens should now be allowing themselves to be impregnated with the deplorable present-day virus of "grab".

It is to be hoped that wiser counsels will prevail and that these teachers will not lower the dignity of their profession by descending to Ned Kelly rules, which seem to be the order of the day in most economic circles.

WAR VIA BACTERIA

If you needed something to worry about, and had tired of bomb blasts and radiation, try some readily available bacterial warfare. .

Letters, S E Wright. The statement by Sir Macfarlane Burnet, that "any attempt to initiate epidemics amongst enemy personnel would be fruitless", should not be taken by readers to mean that **bacteriological warfare** is impracticable.

In fact there does not seem to be any doubt that bacteriological warfare has come to be recognised as a possible potent weapon and investigation into it is being actively pursued.

Brigadier-General William Creasy, Chemical Corps, US Army, whilst deprecating the concept of self-propagating epidemics, has stated that there are real and practical methods of conducting bacteriological warfare and that "**its possibilities are great** – let no one be misled on that score."

CEILING IN DREAM HOMES

Letters, George Molnar. May I join Mr Stafford's plea for reducing ceiling height from 9ft to 8ft, and thus saving millions of pounds in building cost. My only criticism is that he does not go far enough.

Let's face the facts. The average Australian is less than six feet high. Assuming that all the lamps be made flush with the ceiling, and assuming further, that he will refrain from wearing a hat indoors, a six-foot ceiling height can easily be adopted without inconveniencing almost anybody.

But one can go a step further. To determine the ceiling height in relation with a man standing is very wasteful. Surely the different functions of living require different heights. A man sitting does not need more than five feet headroom. For lying in bed or bath four feet is ample. And what about the children's bedroom? We should be able to take advantage of their lesser statures.

I am advocating a type of house with the living-room in the centre, 6 feet high, the roof to slope to 4 feet on either side; where the bedrooms, bath and children's rooms can be suitably arranged.

WOMEN KEEP THE HOME FIRES BURNING

During the War, women found that many activities, that had been restricted to men, were in fact open to them. So that, for example, by 1952 many nice girls were puffing away quite happily on cigarettes in and out of homes. Some of them did this openly, though many of them would not let their mothers or husbands see them, and some of them literally were closet smokers. But in any case, they were now making up a sizeable proportion of the nation's smokers. So now was the time to exploit them.

Men had long been shown in movies smoking non-stop. Did anyone ever see Humphrey Boggart without a cigarette for long? Gregory Peck smoked in a much more sophisticated way, but he was a regular. Now, too, the ladies were all over the silver screen puffing away. Bette Davis, in her bad-girl roles, was a good example. None of them ever resorted to roll-your-own, but every sophisticated lady had to have her ciggie lit for her with a silver lighter.

Locally, the advertising boys of course got on the band wagon. No customer at this stage had any idea of the link between cancer and smoking, so there was no impediment to extravagant claims. Overseas, in Britain and America, the tobacco company executives were getting a hint of harmful links, and were doing their best to suppress them. But over here, it was all marketing without tears. "You never get a sore throat with our brand. Ours is smoother, ours is good for your health, ours will help you lose weight. Light it, you'll like it."

The only exceptions were roll-your-own. These were definitely on the outer. Only the best and most hygienic cigarettes were good enough for you. You have to watch your health.

NEWS AND VIEWS

A number of bush bashers had become lost in the Blue Mountains. Many Letters bemoaned the lack of preparation by some walkers. This Letter below takes the mickey out of some of them, and ends with some sensible advice.

> **Letters, JB, Mosman.** It is surprising that bushwalkers have not yet been advised to equip themselves with native **tom-tom drums**.
>
> These instruments would be invaluable for relaying **Morse Code messages otherwise beaten out on tree stumps.** Moreover, when faced by a precipitous slope, the ardent bushwalker could climb inside his tom-tom and roll over the edge, blowing his **John Peel horn** and firing the **Very Light pistol**, all of which appliances were recommended by previous correspondents.
>
> Restriction cannot curb the eager spirit of the Australian bushwalker. A little care and sense would be worth more than a whole packload of horns or pistols.

JULY: A REALLY SICK ECONOMY

On July 14th, the National Council of wool-selling brokers announced that the Oz wool cheque for 1951 had been half that of 1950. The price-per-pound of wool was also on the downward path, and there were dozens of indicators that this trend had continued into 1952. This suggested that, for a nation riding on the sheep's back, things economic were not too good.

There was plenty of other bad news. For example, wheat plantings for 1952 were down, and were tipped to stay that way in spring, and unemployment was at its highest level for two years. **Well-founded grumblings over the rise in tariffs** and the **import quotas** of a few months ago had never ceased, and now had three months of experience to back them up.

Letters, G Woinarski. Many businesses are finding it impossible to carry on because of Government interference. The law of supply and demand eliminates the necessity for **price control. Import licensing** is to a large extent unnecessary.

Added to this is the impossible position which has arisen owing to the vast number of applications for licences submitted to the licensing authorities and which they are quite unable to cope with.

My company lodged an application on April 28 for the importation of special tools required by Government aircraft factories. An order was placed with the English supplier and the goods had been ready packed since early in May, but my company is unable to establish the necessary letter of credit until a licence is issued. Three months have expired since the date of the application, and we have no licence.

So, business was fighting hard against its own government. But the bad news kept rolling on and on. Worst of all, the Arbitration Court made a new Ruling on the Basic Wage. As you probably remember, this **quarterly** Ruling specified what the Court considered to be the minimum amount of money required to keep a family of **mum and dad and two children** living in reasonable conditions. Each time it was published, it was used as a basis for all the multifarious Trade Unions and bosses to work out what the workers under different awards would be paid. It was all hugely complicated, but it was always true that if the Basic Wage was raised a certain amount, then almost every working adult unionist in the nation got a wage increase of at least that sum.

The Ruling this time was for an increase of 12 Shillings on a Basic Wage of 11 Pounds 15 Shillings. This represented at increase of almost 5 per cent over the June quarter, and suggested **an annual rate of increase of 20 per cent**. Of course, on the one hand, wage-earners were delighted at the big increase in ready cash that they would pocket, but almost immediately this turned to consternation at **the prospect of galloping inflation**. The one thing that the average person in Oz remembered clearly from **the 1920's** was the **ruin and misery that high inflation in Germany** brought to that nation. No one wanted anything like that to happen here.

Likewise employers and large companies **were astounded at the size of the increase.** Up till now, they had viewed with some equanimity the obvious increases in costs on food, clothing and housing, and had thought that, with the economy slowing down, so too would inflationary pressures. But now it was quite clear that such pressures were well and truly loitering, and might well upset apple carts all over the place.

The Letters column sprang to life, with many suggestions on remedies and admonitions.

Letters, W Ashley-Brown (Archdeacon). The further rise in the basic wage should rally all responsible people in defence of our common wellbeing. We cannot afford it.

Many men and women who, through years of hard work and careful living, reared and launched their families and saved enough to secure a modest comfort in their old age. The State had no better citizens. Today they have barely enough to eat. It is no consolation to them to find the streets on Monday mornings littered with empty beer bottles reflecting the luxury untrained youth can now afford.

As an Australian who has served the Empire abroad most of his adult life, I know that many natural fields of trade are denied us because our good friends in many other lands simply cannot afford to trade with us.

A fact I find disconcerting is that we have gifted politicians who, with utter irresponsibility, are content to inch their way to power by promising pleasant things to an unthinking public. If these men persist in doing nothing to avert the threatened disaster, the day of reckoning should mean for them an **indictment of treason before the High Court of Parliament.**

From my experience abroad I believe the time is coming when our possession of unused territory will be justly challenged by land-hungry people.

Our sands are running out. But I do not think it is too late for a national regeneration. Here **religion must be invoked** to play its part. In the meantime let us work harder, live more simply, and love our neighbours more truly.

Comment. The above Letter is interesting. It starts out as moderate enough, then it has a shot at drinking alcohol, then another shot at politicians, with the suggestion that **indictment for treason** might be good enough for them. Finally, it falls back on a cry for a more religious society. This latter plea, stressing the role of religion in creating a better State, was a carry-over from War years where religion was prominent in many Letters. By 1952, the practice of linking religion to some contentious subject was on the decline, but clearly was far from disappearing.

Letters, H Pincas. The bewildering fact of the basic wage rising and money value continuously decreasing recalls similar occurrences in European countries, and shows that history is repeating itself.

In Germany, not so long ago, the Treasurer hit upon the idea that, as prices do not recede voluntarily, they would have to be compelled to; and that wages would follow automatically. So he decreed that, from a certain day, **all prices** – from bread to cars, and from transport to taxes – **had to be cut by 10 per cent.** Two weeks later this operation was repeated. The result was that the next official wage adjustment displayed a recess of about 20 per cent.

Of course, the Government counted upon the obedience to the law and self-discipline of the people – qualities which were abundantly available in **that** country.

Is it as simple as that? "It is," said the learned Dr Schacht, "but most people do not understand the simplicity of economics."

Letters, Wage Earner. The new basic wage increase appears to be a headache to everyone. Certainly no one wants it.

It is obviously impossible for employers to do anything in the matter, but is there any reason why employees could not band together and **refuse to accept the increase**?

Letters, W G F. It seems to me that the present economic muddle is due to the fact that the method of computing the basic wage has been built on false premises.

I understand it is arrived at by an estimate of the cost of living for a married man with a wife and two or three children; and I do not doubt the accuracy of the figures.

But there must be hundreds of thousands of men and single women who are unmarried and who are thus receiving wages for the support of mythical wives and children. I suggest that the basic wage should be arrived at on the cost of living for a single man or woman.

Letters, E Terry. As a salary earner unable to keep pace with rising costs, I wonder why big business does not give a lead by reducing the price of its products.

I have in mind one firm, which has increased its reserves in 10 years from 23,049 Pounds to 639,228 Pounds, and is maintaining a 15 per cent ordinary dividend. Another big corporation maintains a serviced suite, including a cocktail bar, at one of our leading hotels, for those of its directors who visit Sydney. The cost must be 5,000 Pounds a year.

Big furniture retailers insist on a 40 per cent profit. Middlemen selling an expensive refrigerator make a profit of 40 Pounds on each machine without even handling it. A dentist charges from 30 to 60 Pounds for a set of dentures – and the cost of the materials used is not more than 50/-.

Further, in addition to its fantastically high profits of the last decade, big business has provided its hierarchy with luxurious motor cars, liberal "expense" allowances, and other tax-free perquisites.

Do not sane business methods require that those who sell goods shall forgo some of these excessive profits? Then the worker would perforce, and willingly, sell his commodity at a lower figure.

EAT AT LUNCH-TIME? SURELY NOT

Most people reading this will remember the daily six-o'clock swill at the local pubs, all across the nation. The thought of it now, in 2016, still makes every serious and non-serious drinker shudder. But, on working days, the pubs at lunch time were also crowded with men whose very existence was thought to depend on a ration of beer as a means of survival.

This was an era when beer was about the only alcohol consumed by the average man, and many of them took every opportunity they could find to gulp down several quick schooners. So that, when lunch-time came, there were plenty of thirsty customers waiting for service. I mention though that **that service included only the buying of beer, and anyone who wanted to eat needed to go elsewhere**.

The hotels in the large industrial regional city of Newcastle decided that they should go back to **the pre-war practice** of serving **counter lunches, as well as beer, at lunch-time**. So, for a very good price, the drinker could get some bangers and mash, or a meat pie floating in pea soup, and maybe would linger in the pub a bit longer. Then again, a different type of customer, **one who actually liked to eat at lunch-time**, might be enticed.

In any case, many pubs in that fair city started to put them on. Quick as a flash, the Hotel, Club and Restaurant

Employees Union raised objections. They first of all said that the lunches would add to the work of the hotel staff, and hoteliers would have to hire extra staff. Then, in their benevolence, they worried about the nearby restaurants, who might lose trade to the pubs.

Then they worried about public health. "I consider that counter-lunches are unhygienic and encourage excessive drinking, especially in summer. The public probably will have to drink in unhygienic conditions, with refuse scattered around the floors of crowded bars. Counter-lunches disappeared at the start of the War, and we do not want to see them come back."

On the other hand, the Editor of the *SMH* was keen to have them. "Contrary to the view of certain organised housewives, eating will not encourage beer-swilling. A little on-the-spot research would convince the most captious critic that the man munching a meat pie drinks less, and suffers less ill-effects, than the man without. Australia is one of the very few countries in the world where some form of solid nourishment is not provided in better-class bars." He went on to hit the nail on the head. "Even the most supine Australian must rebel against an attempt to **make his drinking-habits the subject of Union rules**."

The Union had a response.

Letters, F Davis, Secretary, HCRE Union of NSW.
It appears that there is a genuine demand by some sections of the public for counter lunches. If these are to become a normal part of hotel business we are of the opinion that the methods adopted by such hotels in Sydney as the Hotel Astra, Bondi, where additional staff and special equipment have been introduced, set

a standard of hygiene and service that could well be the pattern of the industry.

We are opposed to such service if it means that, in addition to the normal onerous duties of bar staff at rush periods, the extra burden of selling foodstuffs over the bar counter would be imposed.

Newcastle Trades and Labour Council, in opposing counter lunches, commented on unsatisfactory conditions of Newcastle hotels rendering them unsuitable for counter lunch service.

Comment. As usual in a dispute, the real issue was not discussed. It was, as was often the case, about money. Could the Union get more payments for its members if they served lunches? It might seem that such payment would be fair, and that the matter could be easily settled by a few tough discussions. But bosses and Unions were not into discussions, they were all set for confrontation. That's why there were so many strikes plaguing the population every day. Workers would walk off the job at the drop of a hat, and bosses would suspend workers for this and for that breach of regulations or protocols.

In any case, a few days later, the Union and hotels jointly announced that the plan had fallen through by mutual consent, and that "the normal friendly and unhurried hygienic service of the past would be continued."

After about two years, some big Sydney hotels **did** start to offer this service, with bar workers being paid an allowance for participating. Within five years, most pubs across the nation were doing the same.

CAN OUR CHILDREN TAKE IT?

At the current time, in the year 2017 say, some of us oldies make snide remarks about the capacity of the younger generation to tough out hard times. Many people think the baby-boomers had it too soft, and were badly spoiled. Others think that the undoubtedly greater physical hardships of earlier times were somehow good for sufferers. These thoughts, though, **were not restricted to the current oldies.** In 1952, there developed a considerable Press conversation on the matter.

Letters, Eileen Straty. Why all the talk about four feet of snow at Kosciusko?

I was born in Nimmitabel. My brother and I used to walk 3¼ miles each way to school from the time I was eight years of age, and we had to walk along a wire fence for nearly a quarter of a mile of this distance to prevent ourselves being buried in the snow.

I still have my quarterly reports showing that I never missed a day and was never late once. What is wrong with the new generation?

Letters, Winifred V Ritchie. I heartily endorse Eileen Straty's letter of July 15. My father, the late E G Williams, was in charge of the Public school at Nimmitabel for 14 years and every morning in the winter he had to dig at least four feet of snow away from the door of the school. Two pupils (twin girls aged nine) used to walk four miles to school and back home every day, and I doubt if they were ever absent.

Find me the school pupil today who would (or could) walk eight miles a day.

Letters, J Mosman. The rigorous childhood existence of the past generation would seem to have achieved very little. I suggest that more emphasis on brain and less on brawn would be a step in the right direction. We have yet to see that the present generation of bus-riding children will be any more inefficient than their snow-ploughing forbears.

Letters, Kathleen Williams. The difficulty is not so much to find a child willing to walk long distances, but to find the parents able to keep such children shod, with present-day extortionate prices and poor-quality leather. The best-quality shoes obtainable would not last a week on our rough country roads. What happens now to the good-quality leather one could rely upon buying prewar?

Letters, Michael Palmer. My recollection is that boys and girls of tender years were so tired when they reached the classroom after long walks to school that the teachers had to batter the "three R's" into them.

Certainly this was one of the reasons why the cane or strap was continually in use in those bad old days.

I invite those of your readers who are prescribing walking feats as a tonic for the rising generation to look at any photograph of a school group of 30 or 40 years ago. If they will do so through the eyes of parents rather than taxpayers, they must be struck by the dull, apathetic faces, in comparison with the alert, smiling, and intelligent children of today.

Letters, Robert Thomson. As an ex-teacher of 51 years' service, I feel that I can speak with some confidence on the subject of pupils' reaction to long walks to school.

In the Inverell district a girl walked four and a half miles to my school. She began her school life at seven years of age and finished at 15. During the whole of that time she never missed one day, which I consider a record. She was the brightest child in that school.

There were other instances of bright pupils who walked long distances to school. Not once did I find that these walks interfered with their school work. It was just a matter of leaving home at a reasonable time.

Comment. A personal memory. These Letters remind me of my own experiences, that were typical of the **country districts** about this time. My primary education was at a convent school of 100 boys and girls in a small mining town in the Cessnock coalfields. The town was poor, and the people were poor. No one had a car, so children walked or biked to school on gravel roads. The average travel distance was two miles, but in keeping with many, many small towns in the nation, most of them turned up each day bare-footed.

This did not depend on the weather. It could be pouring down in a classical Maitland flood, or fields could be under an inch of ice in a black frost. No matter what, most students turned up with no shoes and socks. I do not think it was a deliberate policy of parents trying to save money. It was just that kids liked to go bare-foot, and that **everybody did it**. It was, in effect, part of the otherwise non-existent school uniform.

Of course, it was all different in the cities and larger country towns. Some of these places had school uniforms and even ties and boaters. I can remember on Saturday arvos at the flickers that whenever a newsreel showed these kids in their uniforms, the whole theatre howled with laughter. It was a classic case of reverse snobbery, and just brings back the huge gap that then existed between the wealth of the cities and the poverty of many working-class country towns.

A LETTER ON ABORIGINES

Letters, Michael Sawtell. A man in the Northern Territory was sentenced for being a "combo," which is a bush word for **a white man who lives with or habitually consorts with aboriginal women.**

It is quite right to punish white men who give aboriginal women alcohol, but foolish and puritanical to punish them for being "combos." **The consorting of white men and coloured women has occurred all through history**, and will continue, no matter what any law may declare. Moreover, the law to prevent white men from consorting with aboriginal women can never be satisfactorily enforced.

I know many instances where aboriginal women were splendid mates to their "combo" lovers, and in most instances the half-caste children of these unions were well brought up, and have grown up good Australians, who helped to defend and develop the north.

On my tours in the inland I always make a special study of this problem, and I have been wonderfully impressed by what is being done for these half-caste children in the schools, and generally they are beautiful children.

It is perhaps – but not always – degrading for a white man to consort with an aboriginal woman, but **it may be a great lift up for the woman.** Moreover the beautifully trained and now detribalised young women from the mission stations hope to marry or to become the de facto wives of white men.

The official policy for aboriginal welfare is now all over Australia **assimilation**, but how can the aborigines be assimilated without the aid of the "combos"? Also it is well known that not much can be done towards educating the full bloods to understand citizenship, but it is much easier to both educate and assimilate the mixed bloods.

AUGUST: I CAN JUMP TURNSTILES

Sid Barnes was an Australian cricketer. He regularly opened Australia's batting and, since the War, had starred in several memorable innings. One in particular always came to mind, and that was his 234 with Don Bradman in a Test Match in Sydney in 1946. Bradman also scored 234 in that match and it was often speculated that Barnes threw his wicket away on that exact same score because he did not seek to beat The Don's effort.

Last season, the Oz Cricket Board of Control had seemed to be willing for Barnes to emerge from retirement, to play in the Third Test against the West Indies. But then they dropped him from the Third and subsequent Tests. This absolutely sudden exclusion caught all cricket-lovers by surprise, and was not explained at all by the Board, and **was thus regarded as high-handed and dictatorial**, as well as being a bad selection mistake.

A Mr Raith wrote a Letter at the time to Sydney's *Daily Mirror*, and made comments that implied that Barnes had brought this situation on himself through his actions. Barnes then sued Mr Raith for defamation. In August of 1952, the Court brought down its ruling. It found in favour of Barnes, and awarded costs against Mr Raith. Barnes did not seek damages from him, because he regarded the case simply as a public forum that would make the public realise that the Board had acted prejudicially towards him, without due regard to facts.

So, the thinking of the Board remained a mystery. It appears though that Barnes, a forceful character, first got the Board offside in 1947 in an incident at the Sydney

Cricket Ground. On that day, Barnes had arrived at the Ground only to discover that he had left his Players Pass at home. The attendant manning the turnstile would not let him pass through without paying, and Barnes **had jumped the turnstyle and proceeded to the Players Room.** The attendant had reported the incident to the Board, so Barnes was in hot water, and was officially rebuked by the Board. It was a trivial incident, which the stuffy Board might well have ignored. But in any case, Barnes showed no contrition at all, and thus the Board doubtless felt that he was a player who needed to be watched.

In 1950-51, while on the Oz Tour of England, he had further blotted his copybook. On one occasion, he had apparently persuaded spinner Toshack to leave the rest of the team that was watching play, and both had gone for a game of tennis. Under investigation, it appears that the court was only 50 feet away, so the danger of Toshack not being ready to bat was nil. So, again, the damage done was actually negligible, but the **non-compliance with Rules** loomed large.

Another straw was added at Lords on the same tour. Then Barnes, an amateur cameraman, had gained Lord Gowrie's permission to film King George VI who was watching play. The King was reportedly "delighted" by the idea. But it turned out, most likely to Barnes' surprise, that somebody else had the film rights at Lords, so Barnes had again blotted his copybook. Barnes said repeatedly that he would not have filmed had he known. But the incident added another black mark against him.

Returning now to the Court case, after the Court had heard that **the Board would offer no further evidence** as to the reasons for Barnes' exclusion, Mr Raith apologised profusely for the presumptions in his Letter, and withdrew his defence of truth. The matter was then settled by conference, and as the judge stated, "Mr Barnes's name is cleared."

Letter, G Abbott. The Board, in these days of amateur cricket in Australia, is intent on maintaining the image of Cricket as the whitest of white sports. Player indiscretions are not talked about and player selections are not discussed. In the Barnes case, it had not been able to suppress the news of the turn-style incident, which made headlines for weeks at the time. But the other two improprieties hardly made the News until the Court Case.

In all, though, and given the worthiness of its motives, the Board came out of Barnes affair very badly. It exposed itself to claims that it was petty, bore foolish grudges, had bad judgement, and was prepared to sacrifice Australia's chances in the Tests simply to satisfy those grudges.

I suppose it is too much to ask that these inarticulate men make a public apology to Sid Barnes.

Comment. One Member of the Board, a Mr Johnston, got close to the real reasons for the sacking. In the Court hearings, he said that Barnes was considered "temperamentally unsuitable". This of course covers a multitude of conditions, and generally would mean that a series of small niggles had built up until the camel's back had broken.

PERHAPS BARNES DID STIR THE POSSUM?

Barnes however was always a difficult person to deal with, and had a shrewd eye on his own personal fortunes. On his way back from London with the 1948 Tour, he received information that Customs were waiting to grill him in Sydney about the reported hoard of goods that he would import with him on his return. Accordingly, he left the ship at Melbourne and did not rejoin it, and so missed Customs in those days when dodges were much easier. Also, for example, when he was not playing for Australia, he wrote a regular column for the Daily Mirror, called *"Like It or Lump It",* in which he was always critical of Cricket's Administration, and also the conduct of a few players.

His swan-song to cricket was later in 1952. He was selected for the NSW match against South Australia, but volunteered to play Twelfth Man. So when drinks-breaks came round, it was his duty to carry drinks, and all sorts of whatnots, out on to the field for the other players. He made a fine job of that, but it seems he overdid it. He appeared from the Stands, dressed not in the **traditional creams of a Twelfth Man**, but in a full Business Suit, immaculate with tie, leather shoes and sunnies. He carried with him the drinks as usual, but added cigars, iced towels, a mirror and comb, a radio, and clothes brush. It was a complete and deliberate parody, and after that he was selected only once more for NSW.

Barnes had a **Test Average** (over 19 innings) of 63. His average against England was 71. This is pretty good, given that pitches were of poor quality, and uncovered.

ANTHONY EDEN'S SECOND MARRIAGE

A few times in this book I have indicated that some things never change. But here below I give you some Letters from 1952 that show that **some things have changed**

enormously. In this case, it is **the attitude of Oz society to marriage and divorce**.

The specific occasion that promoted the Letters below was the re-marriage of England's Foreign Minister, Anthony Eden, to the niece of Winston Churchill. Eden had been previously married, and had been granted a decree nisi on the grounds of his first wife's desertion.

Now, he had remarried, and the *Anglo-Catholic Church Times* had editorialised against him doing so. This weekly newspaper was an organ of the High Church of England, and expressed the views of that Church. It said "A generation or so ago, a Foreign Secretary would have felt compelled **to choose between his public career and such a marriage**. Mr Eden's action shows how far the climate of public opinion has **changed for the worse**. It is now apparently to be accepted as a matter of course that those who occupy the highest positions in political and public life may **break the Church's law without embarrassment or reproach.** This act may **make divorce respectable in the eyes of a pagan generation**. But it does not make it one whit the more right."

The Rev A Bunn, vicar of Mr Eden's home Church, however, took a more tolerant view, and called for a more charitable way of dealing with remarriage of divorced people. "While preserving the ideals of the Christian marriage of one man to one woman to the exclusion of all others, there must be a more charitable way of dealing with hard cases other than by insisting on a literal interpretation of Christ's words. Very often a second marriage has the manifest blessing of God. I am not advocating easy divorce, but the whole question had to be approached in a spirit of charity." I dare to say that Rev Bunn, while clearly more sympathetic to Mr Eden, still had a foot in both camps.

The dispute carried over into Australia. The C of E's Dean, Dr Barton Babbage, initially said mildly, but tellingly, that Mr Eden's marriage was **a regrettable lapse** by one who was playing a distinguished and responsible part in public life. The Editorial-writer of the *SMH*, on the other hand, kicked in and did not mince his words. "It would be a bad day indeed if an **overweaning Puritanism were able to drive from public office** men and women, who, in their private lives, were seeking with dignity and sincerity to redress an earlier domestic misfortune."

Letters, Victor Bell. Mr Eden might feel that his marriage is entirely his own private business; and, since it is sanctioned by the laws of the State, his own life is clean, and his service to the community of outstanding value, he might well ask: What right has the Church to exalt **its** laws above the laws of the nation?

The time has long since passed when a great body of churchmen should have recast their view of divorce; for, as everyone knows, much greater evils often arise from the enforced continuance of a partnership, in which love has died, than would be likely to mar a new beginning.

No one would wish to see divorces more common than they are, but it should not be overlooked that when a couple cease to love each other, they are already divorced, whether they appeal to a Court or not.

Letters, S Barton Babbage, Dean of Sydney. It is asserted that Mr Eden's remarriage is his private affair. But Mr Eden is not merely a private citizen, he is also a distinguished Public servant. It is of the essence of our democratic faith that the actions of those who occupy high public office should be subject to public scrutiny and moral judgment. And because life cannot be lived in watertight compartments, it follows that all a man's actions, in so far as they are public, are bound to be critically reviewed.

Letters, A Turner. Criticisms by some church papers and church leaders of Mr Anthony Eden's remarriage was written with more restraint and charitable recognition of different points of view than I think the circumstances call for.

Any criticism of a marriage, performed in accordance with the law of the land, (as Mr Eden's was), **should be a ground for an action for defamation.** Such a law would have a salutary effect on people who describe a lawful marriage as "a regrettable lapse."

Letters, Divorcee. In all the views proffered concerning Mr Eden's divorce and remarriage I have seen no reference to the rights of the second Mrs Eden.

Mr Eden may or may not be justified in his action, but I question the right of the Church to deny fulfilment of Mrs Eden's love. In this case, the attitude of the Church has dimmed a little what should have been the brightest day of Mrs Eden's life.

I know from personal experience that the memory of such an incident persists.

Letters, Victor Bell. I still contend that many churchmen are too rigid and backward in their views of marriage and divorce. Although in celebrating a wedding the formula – "Those whom God hath joined together let no man put asunder" – is used, who could believe that every first marriage is divinely sanctioned and approved?

Does God join an unconfessed impotent man to a healthy woman? Is a wife bound to endure the cruelty and brutality of a drunken husband? Or a husband to put up with a wife who gads about and neglects home and children? To say that marriages of this kind are "made in heaven" is unethical nonsense.

Many churchmen and others are doing splendid work in guiding young folk into sensible marriages. Of these it might be said "God hath joined them together" and they will never want to be "put asunder".

Letters, S Barton Babbage. On the matter of divorce, the laws of the State diverge and differ from the laws of the Church. The Church recognises, of course, the legality of civil marriage and the full power of the State to enact its own laws. The Church believes, however, that the laws of the State in this matter have departed from the Christian ideal, and it insists, therefore, on different standards for its own members. That is why, in my original comment, I said: "It was impossible for the Church to solemnise Mr Eden's marriage because it conflicted with Christian convictions concerning the sacredness of the marriage bond."

Dr Bell asks a number of rhetorical questions: "Does God join an unconfessed impotent man to a healthy woman?" Of course not. The answer of both Church and State is that such a marriage is null and void. "Is a wife bound to endure the cruelty and brutality of a drunken husband?" Of course not. The answer is that separation is possible.

It would help clarity of discussion if statements were not gratuitously attributed to me. It would then be unnecessary to accuse me of talking "ethical nonsense". I never asserted, for example, that all marriages were "made in heaven". Many marriages, it is only too clear, are entered into "unadvisedly, lightly, or wantonly". But Christian marriage, rightly understood, is **a lifelong and indissoluble union.**

BUILD A BETTER BUTTER-BOX

Harry Seidler was an architect, of Austrian parentage, born in 1923, and was now living in Canada. He came to Australia to design a house for his parents, and it was **this house** that in mid-August won the prestigious John Sulman Medal, one of Australia's most important architectural prizes. At the time, and later, he was quite outspoken on the worth of Australia's architecture. Whether it was our houses or our public buildings, he had **something** to say.

"Houses here are obvious for their all-consuming timidity. People can't think of anything except bricks, tiles, and little windows. This is a southern country. We can use colour and light. We can build homes along clean and simple lines right through to the last ash-tray.

"The new Maritime Services building is an utter disgrace. I can't find words strong enough to describe it. It's terribly expensive and ornamental. A classic exterior, copying old Greece or Rome, was the main object. It's utterly decadent.

"Official Government architecture in Australia is really criminal. The typical Housing Commission bungalows and blocks of flats are an outrage. The Housing Commission's blocks of flats at North Sydney are named after Francis Greenway. This is a great insult to a man who did some quite good things here."

Such fighting words were unlikely to endear Mr Seidler to many practising architects, so his remarks opened up quite a controversy.

Letters, Ajax.   In an article on the winner of the John Sulman Medal for architecture, your Staff Correspondent refers to Mr Harry Seidler as quietly spoken and courteous. I fail to detect courtesy to his confreres in his scathingly contemptuous references to Australian architecture. "Utter disgrace," "utterly decadent, "all-consuming timidity" are examples.

This young man is certainly not lacking in assurance. It seems that after intensive search he has discovered "one healthy little building in Sydney." How nice of him to concede this! His reference to "shacks" is rather bewildering, considering that his much-discussed design – a glamorised aviary – conforms to the generally accepted conception of a "shack."

Mr Seidler's record of academic achievements is impressive. Let us hope his work is compatible with his erudition. In the meantime, search in Sydney may reveal to him examples of architecture which are worthy of emulation or adaptations to modernity.

Letters, N W McPherson, ARAIA. Mr Seidler is to be congratulated on his contribution of new thoughts. That is always healthy and provocative. But the final test of functional thought design is: How far is it truly functional? There is no point in creating something different just because it is different, unless it achieves a real advance in purpose and beauty.

Climate in a given country is the most important factor in the design of its homes. Our sunny days lead some to liken our climate to "Mediterranean." But we have to face it – there is hardly a climate more precocious. It is a climate of extremes of heat and cold; of winds sometimes high and dry, sometimes driving lashing rain; of summer calms heavy with sticky heat. The days are few to which we would care to throw wide our homes and enthusiastically say, "Come in and sit down."

Do flimsy wooden walls, hundreds of square feet of glass, and elevated floors underneath which the wind can whistle, and roofs only a few inches above one's head constitute the answer? There is a deep sense of security and stability offered by stout walls on good foundations, roofs insulated by a sufficient air space, and windows that have a rational relationship to climate as it really is.

The flat roof has its uses but it is of no functional value except to walk and sit out on. If provision for these purposes is not incorporated in the plan, it is likely to look harsh and dull. Imagine looking down from Livingstone Avenue, Pymble, on an array of bituminous felt roofs! Personally, I much prefer the present view of soft shapes and tonings among the trees. It is also likely to give a box-like appearance to the house.

Mr Seidler says he does not like our brick boxes but I remember in my University days being warned against "butter-box architecture." If we must have boxes (and I don't see why we should) it is questionable whether a brick box is not preferable to a wooden one.

Letters, Interested Housewife. After inspecting Mr Seidler's prize-winning house at Turramurra I would like to ask those of my sister housewives who have seen it three questions:

Were you impressed by the rotary clothes line which is so much in view as you approach the house? How would you like to cook a hot meal on a summer's afternoon in the kitchen with its unprotected wall facing west? Do you suspect that the judges, in awarding the medal to this residence, were carried away by the spectacular, which is very pleasing to the occasional glance, but becomes tiresome to live with?

Letters, J K Farley. The old adage, "truth hurts," is certainly proving true now. Australians don't like to be reminded that they are half a century behind the times in architectural design. I only hope that Mr Seidler does not become discouraged before he converts rut-loving Australians.

Letters, H L Rudd. This year's winner of the John Sulman Medal for architecture would only get a wooden spoon for good manners. His attack on a body of men who are evolving a style of architecture suitable to Australia and the Australian people is equalled only by his ignorance of the many fine modern houses at present in existence in Sydney's suburbs.

I can only assume that his tirade was uttered with his tongue in his cheek to induce his fellows to copy the modern or futuristic trend. He has, however, succeeded only in antagonising people.

Letters, F M Cowper, FRAIA. I believe the public is becoming more and more confused by the various arguments put forward by architects and others in discussing the Sulman award.

While there is nothing wrong with large windows, it seems obvious that the Seidler house with extensive areas of glass walls is only suitable for a large site in which the house can be built well within its own grounds, thereby preserving some privacy for the occupants.

Another consideration is that this type of building is far more expensive than the normal orthodox type.

Flat roofs were the fashion 30 years ago, but have been avoided as far as possible by discriminating architects on account of the excessive and continual cost of maintenance and repair.

Further, glass walls, to be comfortable, require to be double thickness or otherwise specially treated. Alternately, some form of mechanical ventilation or air conditioning is necessary, which again means added cost for this type of house.

Comment. Mr Seidler must have found a suitable house to inhabit in Sydney, because he stayed here and prospered. He remained controversial throughout his life, and his work is either loved or hated by observers. Among his creations was the Australia Square project, at the time the world's tallest light-weight concrete building. He also designed our most reviled building, the Blues Point Tower, on the foreshores of Sydney Harbour. During his life, he received five Sulman Awards, as well as awards from many International and National Architecture Institutes, and was made a Companion of the Order of Australia.

PENSIONER'S RATES

Letter, (Ald) G Carruthers. The decision to postpone the debts of needy pensioners shows that municipal and shire Councils are tackling a community problem that is not rightly theirs.

The State Government's offer to refund half the amount concerned only applies to aged pensioners. Not to invalids, widows or war veterans. They also apply only to home owners. No suggestion has been made to refund rents. If the Government's principle is sound, then it must surely legislate to give some equitable relief to all pensioners.

NEWS AND VIEWS

Letters, A Victim. It is pleasing to learn that the Government proposes to amend the Local Government Act to give municipal councils power over private tennis courts. For too long councils have been powerless to prevent the operation of **night tennis courts** for hire in residential areas.

Neighbours have had to put up with the noise and lights until 11p.m. If they tried to sell their homes they found that the proximity of the night court reduced the value of the property. Such courts should be classified as business or industrial premises and banned from residential areas.

Letters, Another Victim. "A Victim's" letter on the need for control of night-tennis courts gave me great satisfaction.

This correspondent could have said much more. He could perhaps have mentioned having his doorbell rung at 11.25p.m. (after trying for more than an hour to get to sleep) and being asked to get a ball. Sometimes you can't help laughing at their nerve.

The proposed legislation is long overdue.

WOULD YOU LIKE A SMALL WAGER?

It is Saturday afternoon and you want a bet on the races. You are in a small country town, two hundred miles from the nearest race track where you can legally get a bet. What can you do?

You can walk into the nearest pub. There you will find two bookies, one out near the dunny, and the other in the Ladies Parlour. I suggest you go the Parlour because it smells less than the other one.

Walk up to a fat rude man who is a non-stop smoker. Show him your money and say you want a bet. If you are a man and appear able-bodied, he will ask you if you are a cop. If you say no, he will believe you, and ask for your cash. Once he has that, he will take your bet. He will offer you the odds he gets from the phone, **or** the Starting Price odds. After that, you are mates for life.

If you lose, go in and have a schooner before the beer runs out. If you win, the pay-out is immediate. Check your notes for duds. But have a schooner any way.

SEPTEMBER: BUILDING IN WOOLLAHRA

Woollahra was one of Sydney's wealthiest suburbs, the home of the rich and famous. Not the rich and famous world of show-business people or sports stars, but solid dependable types like lawyers, bankers, and even the occasional entrepreneur. As such, the houses built there were stolid and dependable, often of many years standing or, if they were new, it was expected that they would be of conservative design. The local Council was quite at home with this very respectable mood, and sought to enforce it on dwelling **applications**.

Hence this Letter, which arose when an applicant wanted to build a house with **a lime-tallow wash over common bricks**.

Letters, John Moore, of Moore, Walker and Croaker, Architects, Sydney. Our plans for a small cottage were recently submitted to the Woollahra Council for their approval. This was given subject to certain conditions, one of which said: "All external walls to be of **face bricks or common bricks cement rendered**." That is, not the lime-tallow wash we requested.

This is the reply of small men of authority when they do not know the answer. The architect fully trained and experienced in his profession is denied the exercise of a particular design expression, by a group of men with little knowledge of architecture.

To colour-wash or not to colour-wash a wall of common bricks is in itself a small matter, one of preference for the designer concerned – no more than that. But for a body of laymen to dictate a matter of design, peculiarly the concern of the trained professional, and on top of that to sidestep the request for a reason is anything but a small matter.

It is a gross impertinence.

Municipal councils do excellent work, and the community would be poorer indeed without their help and control, but they should keep to matters of which they have knowledge and experience, and not trespass beyond these.

Letters, L Robinson, Double Bay. I would point out to Mr John Moore that the Woollahra aldermen have been elected to represent the majority of the residents and house owners of that municipality, and **not the architects**.

They have done so to the satisfaction of the electors for many years and have created a fine residential district. I would hate to have a "lime and tallow tinted" house put up next to mine. I have noticed that this treatment is generally used for cow sheds and dairies in this country.

Letters, W Harvey, Mayor, Municipality of Woollahra. Mr John Moore takes the Woollahra Council to task because the council in discharging a statutory duty, imposed upon it by the Local Government Act, when considering his plans for a dwelling, has differed from him in what is regarded as the proper external finish on a building in a high-class residential locality.

On valuable land, now assessed at almost 80 Pounds a foot, Mr Moore specified that the walls of the dwelling should be of common bricks, painted with lime and tallow-tinted cream. The council has not been satisfied with the durability of this finish and therefore attached a condition of approval requiring the use of face bricks, or, if common bricks were desired, then they should be **cement rendered** instead of **lime washed**. These conditions were accepted by the applicant and the specifications were altered accordingly.

After a lapse of over 12 months, the architect commenced the preparation of the building for **lime washing**, contrary to the amended specifications. A notice to discontinue this work was served on the builder.

Mr Moore omits to mention in his letter that he neglected to comply with the terms of the council's approval. There is no question of a "Dictatorship in House Design." Architects and builders know that they have the right of appeal against any decision of a council. Mr Moore did not see fit to exercise his right.

Letters, J Newsom. Mr Moore has his normal democratic right to protest in public. His standing as an architect, and also as an artist, should be sufficient assurance of his professional judgment that the house, as he proposed it, would have been in good taste. On the other hand the council's competence in the matter is open to question.

To use facebricks or cement rendering on the outside walls will not ensure freedom from shabbiness. Acres of dirty and shabby brickwork and cement rendering testify to that.

For generations, whitewash (lime over commons) has been good enough for the outside of the **White House, Washington**, and of the home of many another persons of lesser eminence. It should be good enough for Woollahra.

Letters, F Wallis. Alderman Harvey has stressed the very point which would appear to be the cause of frustration to professional men and injustice to their clients, namely that the only right of appeal against a Council's decision is to a Court of Law.

An appeal of this sort entails a very long delay, impossible to the average homebuilder or sub-divider and the possibility, with further appeals, of a financial commitment completely beyond the means of the average person.

Letters, John Bambach, Vaucluse.   Some of the facades of Sydney's civic squares are hideous – even though the individual buildings contained therein are quite pleasing in themselves. This is due to the fact that there has been no authoritative body controlling the proper massing of architectural features.

Much the same sort of condition can occur in a neighbourhood; and a modern individualistic home should reasonably be frowned upon if it is to "scream," through incompatibility, at the established development in the area.

Most parts of the Woollahra municipality possess a distinct and pleasing pattern in buildings and gardened cartilage – the work of councils over many years, which rightly should be protected.

If architects want to lead and reform Woollahra and other Local Government authorities, they could play a useful part from within, as aldermen – not as injured critics from outside, in aloof technical bodies.

SHOPPING HOURS

Prior to the War, in various States, some shops of various sizes were allowed legally to stay open on Thursday or Friday nights, and also perhaps on Saturday mornings. When the War came, most shops and service stations opened at eight or nine in the morning and closed about five or six in the evenings. Now, in 1952, an argument was raging about whether extended shopping hours should be allowed.

The Trade Unions representing shop assistants were opposed to this, because it meant the workforce would be called on to work different hours, in abnormal shifts. This might open up the scope for non-Union people to take Union jobs. **Shop owners** supported the longer hours because they saw them as likely to increase profits. **Customers** also supported more opportunity for convenient shopping. **Shop assistants** on the whole **liked** the idea of more hours, **but at penalty rates**, and did not like the extra hours on their feet. In all, it was a mixed bag, and claims and counter-claims flew back and forth.

Letters, (Mrs) Kathleen Jensen. The secretary of the NSW Retail Traders' Association, Mr J Griffin, is reported as having said in regard to the late closing **ballot** for shop assistants that "it might be much better for Alderman O'Dea to take a poll to ascertain **the wishes of shoppers**." There was a similar outcry when it was suggested that butchers' shops close on Saturday morning. **Thoughtful housewives shop intelligently, arranging their purchases with a minimum of inconvenience to those who supply their needs.**

Shop assistants give good service and deserve greater consideration. They are the Cinderellas of industry. Their Saturday is completely spoiled by having to put in three to four hours pandering to customers **who are in the main selfish housewives.**

Letters, James Griffin, Retail Traders' Association of NSW. Mrs Kathleen Jensen shows a refreshing consideration for shop assistants, which we appreciate and so will they, without doubt. The necessity for them to work on Saturday morning is irksome, but shopping facilities are nothing if not a service to the community and, as such, should be available at all reasonable times.

One wonders how far Mrs Jensen carried her consideration. Does she, for example, not use public transport after 5pm during the weekends, so that the people employed in these occupations may also enjoy the same standard working hours as the whole community?

On this line, how far does she want to take it? Would it, for example, suit her **for the whole city**, and all activities in it, including the police force, **to shut down at 5.30pm each day**, and for the whole weekend, until 9am on Monday, and would she include with that electricity services, gas services, and water services in addition to transport and places of entertainment?

With respect to her comments on butchers' shops, it is realised that the food requirements of the household are largely the responsibility of **the housewife who can shop at almost any time.** That is not true, though, for business people and workers in industrial areas shopping for clothing needs; engaged couples and home-makers seeking furniture, etc.

Letters, K Hutchinson. Mr James Griffin, secretary, Retail Traders' Association of NSW, while agreeing that Saturday trading is irksome for shop assistants, offers no solution to their problem and seeks to divert attention from the issue by citing the position of workers in transport and similar essential services.

Such employees are classified as shift workers, and accordingly receive penalty rates for night work and weekend work, including Saturday mornings. Shop assistants do not receive penalty rates for Saturday morning work.

As a member of the public, may I suggest that the retail traders and the shop assistants approach the government with the request that Friday night trading be reintroduced in lieu of Saturday morning for a trial period of, say, six months.

Letters, Phyllis Parkinson. Friday night shopping was an ideal opportunity for shoppers. Today, thousands of women are denied the chance of sharing with their husbands the many pleasant, and expensive, decisions involved in fitting and maintaining a home.

Shop assistants are not Cinderellas referred to by Mrs Jensen who regard every working hour as a robbery of their leisure, but intelligent people selling their services and protected against exploitation. Today they need neither righteous champions nor inflexible and restrictive Acts of Parliament, but rather a chance to justify their salaries by working efficiently and competitively when they are needed most.

In this climate, it is inevitable that some shops will test the Law to see if it will be enforced. After all, the laws on drinking in hotels and for SP betting were almost completely ignored. Maybe after-hours shopping will get the same treatment.

News item, September 13. A shopkeeper in Neutral Bay, Mr Eggars, selling modernistic furniture, stayed open until 9 pm last night, a Friday, instead of closing at the mandated 5.30 pm. In the first hour, he was approached by two men who identified themselves as Messrs Campbell and Murphy for the Shop Assistants Union, and they stated that the shop was supposed to close at 5.30 pm.

The shopkeeper replied that he intended to stay open. He explained that he did not employ anyone, and was not a member of a Trade Union.

The Union Reps indicated that it did not matter, and that he could do all of his business in normal trading hours. The reply was that it was not possible, and that people rang him night after night asking him to open up for them. The Reps then indicated that he was doing something that had not been done before, and he replied that it was about time someone did it. The Reps said they would report him, and added that their concern was that other shops in the area **with** Union staff might be tempted to stay open as well. At 9 pm, the shopkeeper had trouble clearing his shop to close. He said he saw more people last night than he would normally see in a fortnight.

News item, September 15. The Minister for Labour and Industry, Mr F Finnan, said that Mr Eggars and all others who stayed open outside of legal trading hours, would certainly be prosecuted. He said that "hours of trading have been fixed by the Industrial Commission. If people disregard this law they will meet the same fate as hundreds of others who have already been prosecuted. Whether offenders are small storekeepers or big firms, no exception can be made when the law is broken. Until and unless the law is altered, the present law will be carried out in its entirety as it has been over the years."

That seemed to be that for the moment. Only two further Letters on the matter were published in the *Sydney Morning Herald.* Both of them were, I think, further off the point than on it.

Letters, Hester Jesson, Housewives' Association of NSW. Members of my Association have expressed their increasing concern at the reluctance of many shopkeepers, now that **wartime shortages of wrapping paper** are over, to wrap their wares properly. In many shops where food is sold, the basic requirements of hygienic wrapping are often ignored, and breaches of the Pure Food Act committed. What is more, I've yet to meet the woman who enjoys coping with a parcel wrapped in old newspaper.

This association has written to the Lord Mayor, asking for his support in securing the enforcement of the Act against shopkeepers who seem unable to grasp the idea of service to the customer.

Letters, (Mrs) L Robin. Perhaps it would be far better if shops were to open their doors earlier and close earlier.

If shops were to open at 8.30am each trading day, it would enable office workers to buy various items before commencing work, thus alleviating the nightmare task of shopping, even for quite small items, in their luncheon period.

PROPOSED LAWS ON LEUCOTOMY

On September 16th, the NSW Government announced that it proposed to introduce changes to certain laws relating to a surgical procedure called leucotomy, also called a lobotomy.

In a leucotomy, the surgeon severs the front lobes of the brain from the rest of the brain centres. The operation is performed as a last resort, in otherwise hopeless mental cases, often cases in which the patient is physically violent. Patients receiving this treatment often manifest extreme depression and dislike for other people who, they believe, are persecuting them. Many of them are suicidal.

Proof exists that in many cases leucotomy has effected dramatic improvement in the condition of patients. Their anxiety and worry has ended, and their delusions and violence have been replaced by rational thought and behaviour.

Nevertheless, an element of risk is involved. Critics of the operation have cited cases where the operation has turned the patient into a person so docile and indifferent that he is unable to lead a normal social life. In other cases, where a surgeon has cut too extensively, convulsions have been produced in patients who never previously had them.

The proposed NSW Legislation. The Government wanted to amend existing legislation for the Master of Lunacy to follow. **He already had the power to move insane persons into mental institutions,** and held the duty of guardianship over them. **Now, it was proposed** that he should have the additional power to **force** patients to have a lobotomy, **with or without the consent of the patient, or their relatives or parents.** In doing this, he was to be assisted by a Consultative Committee that would provide the necessary authority. Electro-convulsive therapy was also included in the new Laws.

Letters, Ben Doig. The Cahill Government has signed its own death warrant at the next elections, by approving a bill to permit brain cutting of mental patients, without the consent of parents or relatives.

Other bungling and injustice is insignificant compared with the horror of this proposed Fascist legislation. The totalitarian Cahill Government must be sacked.

Letters, W Grant. By shouting "Fascist" at the Cahill Administration for its proposed legislation relating to leucotomy, it seems to me that your correspondent Ben Doig has reacted in a typically political manner without attempting to form a considered judgment.

The Government's proposition poses most of the problems relating to a consideration of euthanasia, and it is all too easy to avoid careful thought of such matters by appealing to prejudices – religious or political.

Few of us care to condone any infringement of the rights or liberties of the individual, but what liberty has a person who is a slave to ever-present obsessions and compulsions? What right have parents or relatives to withhold consent for an operation which, while not producing a completely normal person, may, at least, relieve a hopelessly insane individual of all the tormenting tension which would otherwise make life a torture of unceasing restlessness.

One realises that legislation of the proposed type is always potentially dangerous, but to condemn it merely because it happens to be the brain-child of one's political adversaries is to prostitute one's intellectual powers.

Letters, E Davidson, St James' Vestry, King Street.

There are good grounds for believing that many unfortunate sufferers may be cured by leucotomy, or the effects of their insanity mitigated. This legislation, however, raises questions that cannot be confined to the level of mental healing or even of the welfare of certain unfortunate individuals.

It compels us to face the whole problem of the danger of **permitting the State**, functioning through approved medical officers or through one Public servant, the Master in Lunacy, **to abrogate the will of the individual**.

This problem is vital to democracy. We cannot afford to ignore this legislation or even to assume that it cannot be abused. It happens to permit an operation on the human body without the consent of the individual or of the nearest relative.

In other words, it invests the State with precisely the same kind of authority employed by the German Government during the Hitler regime when certain physical operations were performed on people for what was considered their own and the State's good. At the time most Germans gave tacit consent to this denial of liberty. They afterwards learnt that precedents, once established, can be broadened till they make tragic inroads on human rights.

I believe that the attempt of the medical profession and the NSW Government to extend the benefits of modern surgery to sufferers from the worst forms of mental complaints is wholly admirable. It proceeds from the most humane motives. But where will this creation of precedent lead? Is it the forerunner of further legislation "for our good"?

What guarantees have we that the State will not legalise other kinds of operations irrespective of the will of the individual? This is indeed "loaded" legislation. It calls for the closest scrutiny.

Letters, S Barton Babbage, Dean of Sydney. But there is a more immediate problem. The proposed bill authorises the operation of leucotomy with or without the consent of the patient concerned or the consent of the next of kin. This is a serious departure from previous medical practice in any other field. It is astonishing that the British Medical Association should have placed its imprimatur upon this proposed clause.

Leucotomy is by no means an infallible cure for mental ills. Some patients, as a result of leucotomy, improve (although some, who improve physically, develops strange amoral and antisocial behaviour characteristics); other patients do not improve, and in a very few cases actually regress.

From the point of view of the Christian faith, a man's personality is his most sacred possession. It is a very serious thing to interfere with and to alter radically the personality of a man.

It may be held that, in a state of chronic mental disturbance, the application of the most drastic remedies is justified. Nevertheless, a person, though insane, has rights: he is still a human being with his own distinctive personality: and that personality should not be forcibly changed without his consent (if he is capable of giving it); or, alternatively, without the consent of his next of kin.

The proposed course has an unpleasant suggestion of totalitarianism. This is the more regrettable, in that the bill, from other points of view, is wholly admirable.

It is to be earnestly hoped that the clause under discussion will be deleted or substantially revised.

Comment. This was a matter that was far from settled. The legislation was still in the draft stage, and pressure was mounting. The Government still had time to change it. Would it do that? Perhaps we will find out next month.

NEWS AND VIEWS

Letters, B H Walsh. Grazier J Macarthur-Onslow's suggestion that "1,000 or so" unemployed should go out into the country and trap rabbits, seems less of a genuine suggestion to help relieve economic distress than **a familiar kick at the industrial and city worker.**

The sneer that rabbiting would entail "work" does him little credit. His letter would have had more worth if he had suggested new ways and means for trappers. It should be recognised that a rabbit, to the average city man, is no more than a newspaper item.

It seems to me that if we persist in this habit of "knocking" each other, the problems that this continent poses for us will largely remain unsolved. It might be an idea to try helping each other. Even if this makes some feel uncomfortably virtuous, there is always the consoling thought that, in the long run, one is helping oneself.

Flight to the moon. Dr Wernher von Braun predicted today that a 50-man expedition of scientists and technicians will land on the moon by 1977. Dr Braun is head of US Army Guided Missiles Development.

He predicted that three rocket ships, each 160 feet long and 110 feet wide, will carry the men. They will take off from a space station erected in an orbit 1075 miles from the earth.

Letters, Victor Bell. It makes me wonder whether Dr Von Braun may, like Daedalus, lose the wings of his vaulting ambition, or be frozen to a lunary fossil, should he ever reach the moon.

What chance of survival would any man have in those opposite extremes without air for breathing or for speaking to his fellow? He might pack a hamper of oxygen and a few synthetic sandwiches, but how long would they last, even for a few men? I would much rather stay here.

Surely it is wrong to spend, as Dr Braun calculates, four thousand million dollars on the first trip to the moon when almost half the population of our own planet is just above the breadline, millions of children are maimed and homeless as the result of our wars, and deadly diseases still clog the wheels of our progress. It will be time to make an excursion to the moon when we have first set our own globe in order, and know how to live in peace and harmony.

Comment. Of course, and I am sure you will all agree, that Doctor Braun is living in fantasy land, and Mr Bell is quite right to bring him down to earth. Every sensible person knows that **man will never travel to the moon**, and that even if he got there, his lungs would balloon out and he would die as soon as he put foot on the surface. Impossible. Ridiculous.

OCTOBER: LAST WORD ON LOBOTOMY

The leucotomy debate was raging on. This first Letter presents a plea that was in favour of the Legislation, though in the case of children, it now argued that parental consent was necessary.

Letters, Irvine Hunter. Should the chance of benefit to an insane person be denied him because of the ignorance, prejudice, irresponsibility or even malice of relatives?

Mental disease still has a considerable social stigma. It might in some cases suit relatives to have the patient remain in a mental hospital instead of having the responsibility thrust upon them of somebody not completely normal, but yet so improved as no longer to require institutional treatment.

In the case of minors, no operation should be allowed without the parents' consent; but so far as concerns insane patients of full age, precluded from giving their own consent only by reason of their illness, it would seem right that the Court should exercise its judgment for them on the same principle which governs it in managing all their affairs, namely, the good of the insane patient alone.

The procedure should be by summons to a District Court Judge in chambers, the relatives being given an opportunity to lodge their objections (if any).

From the judge's decision on the evidence before him, there should in general be no appeal, as it is a pure question of fact that is involved in each case.

But **most of the population were dead set against the new laws.** Even the *SMH* editor got right off the fence. He argued that when a person was certified as insane, it was perfectly obvious that he became a ward of the State, and that his affairs should be managed by the State. But when it came to crucial and problematic medical treatment, **the family must be considered as well.** "The patient is still a member of the family. He is still an individual. No legal form of words can blot out his family's interest in his welfare, or alienate their right to be consulted in all matters affecting it. The justification offered for the totalitarian legislation offered is specious."

Community alarm was expressed by clergy, politicians, and public figures. Letter writers had their say.

Letters, C V Pilcher, St Andrew's Cathedral. The proposed legislation strikes at the dearest rights of human personality.

I will not enlarge on the possible agony of the mental patient in question, but suggest for consideration the pain of the parents when the operation has been forced on a beloved child against their will and has proved to be, as is sometimes the case, a ghastly failure.

Letters, W G Kett. The question of the value of and the necessity for leucotomy is a matter for the neurosurgeon alone.

What is called in question is the wisdom of legislation which establishes an extremely dangerous precedent and ignores human rights.

I was in Germany in 1938 when similar legislation was seriously disturbing thoughtful medical men and sociologists, who saw the possibility for evil in such legislation but, of course, had no opportunity for public discussion.

The benefit of legislation which permitted surgical interference in a wide range of conditions, especially where heredity was involved, irresistibly appealed to specialists in various fields, who were concerned mainly with the medical benefits to the community.

The diabolical results that followed the extension of that legislation are now matters of history.

Among the points raised in favour of leucotomy legislation is that the population of mental institutions would be reduced. **The logical development**, if this point is taken seriously, would be further legislation to reduce the population in other institutions of totally different characters.

All of this type of pressure built up, and **the government finally changed its mind.** On October 14th, it brought down changes that said that if a person was married, then his wife must give permission. Also, that if an adult was not married, his guardian at the time must give permission. And that for a child, the parents must give consent. This new law was subject only to the caveat that if the Master of Lunacy thought that permission was being held back unjustifiably, then he could appeal to the Full Court of NSW.

Comment. The Law was fixed on that basis. As it turned out, at about this time, the bottom fell out of the leucotomy market, because psychiatrists found that certain neuroleptic and antipsychotic drugs appeared to do the same job without the bad results and side effects. Only a handful of patients in NSW received the compulsory treatment. The treatment persisted, on an ever-reducing basis for years however, and more and more on a voluntary basis. By the 1980s, it had died out almost completely, both in Australia and world-wide.

RENTAL RETURNS ON PROPERTIES

Back in **the very early years of WWII**, Federal and State Governments introduced Laws and Regulations that were intended to provide stability in the housing market for an unsettled population. In particular, it introduced Rules that said that **the rents for dwellings must not be increased** unless the landlord made large improvements to the premises. And even then, the landlord was required to front some form of Tribunal and argue the case for an increase. This turned out to be a long, costly, time-consuming and frustrating experience that attracted relatively few.

This measure was accepted with misgivings by landlords across the nation, but given the low inflation and tough austerity in the war-time years, alarm bells tinkled rather than tolled. However, as the War rolled on, and entered its seventh year, and the rules were still in place, landlords started agitating to have the restrictions removed. By 1952, after a dozen years, believe it or not, the original Laws were still in place.

This was, of course, **very popular with the renters**. Wages had increased a lot over that time period, and right now inflation was racing at about 20 per cent. On the other hand, landlords were tearing their hair out, because their rental takings had not increased for 12 years. On top of that, the values of their properties had been rated higher by local Councils, so they were now paying higher rates.

In between the two interested groups were the politicians. It was obvious to all that the whole business was inequitable to landlords. But **they** did not have nearly the same voting power as the tenants. Politicians sat on their hands, and pretended that the Tribunals set up to allow rent increases were in fact working. So, late in 1952, the absurd situation continued.

One obvious consequence of this was that reputable building groups had no incentive to build new dwellings. Who wanted to build a house and rent it at a fair price, but not be able to raise rents as inflation inevitably took its toll? So the result was a shortage of housing, and this would normally have caused rents to rise. But rent rises were forbidden. So the landlords were doubly cursed, they felt.

Letter-writers had a bit to say about all this.

Letters, P L Summers. It is extraordinary that the one thing on which all political parties have for long agreed upon is that rents should not be allowed to rise. I suppose the only explanation can be that there are more tenants than owners.

In June, 1950, I wrote to the "Herald" pointing out that whereas **a landlord could not legally obtain more than a 5 per cent investment on his property**, his tenant could legally sub-let and obtain 20 per cent, without falling foul of the law. Next day the Attorney-General replied agreeing with the complaint I had made and saying that the position would be remedied. Yet that is still the position today – in spite of the fact that I have since written to the Attorney-General more than once reminding him of his promise.

Letters, Yet Another Solicitor. The Government responsible for enacting the Fair Rents Act and for its administration is to be commended, as under that Act both landlord and tenant can obtain a fair deal. If such controls were removed, no doubt thousands of unfortunate tenants would have their rents excessively increased by unscrupulous landlords, and any tenant unable to pay the excessive rent imposed would probably have to defend an action for ejectment, thus causing a further congestion in our courts.

As to assisting speculative builders, no doubt many will agree with me that there are already too many jerry-built homes about Sydney and suburbs erected by that class of builder.

In my opinion rent controls are not the cause of the housing shortage and the Fair Rents Act and controls should be retained.

Letters, P Summers. Every tenant knows perfectly well that the rent he pays is principally based upon a value 10 years old, or more. He apparently considers that a "fair" rent. On that basis, and quite contrary to his contention, he is well aware no landlord can be awarded a fair rent.

He proceeds to speculate upon what would happen if controls were removed, but I did not suggest they should be. My contention was that there would have been no housing shortage had it not been for the Fair Rents and Moratorium Acts. As to jerry-built houses, I do not deny there are such, but their existence is due to the lack of supervision of local councils and shires, which have ample powers. In any case, a jerry-built house is better than none.

Letters, W Swinson. It may well be that if rent controls were removed thousands of unfortunate tenants would have their rents excessively increased by unscrupulous landlords.

But this is no reason why landlords should be singled out for discriminative treatment and, as a result of the Fair Rents Act, be compelled to subsidise the rest of the community.

If it is considered that in the national interest rents should be pegged at the rental values as at August, 1939, then **the State should pay the subsidy**.

If this were done **the cost would be spread over the whole body of taxpayers**, including landlords, and the latter would not be unfairly penalised by having to bear the whole of the cost, which no one with any sense of justice can say is equitable.

Letters, (Rev) R Hickin, St Paul's Rectory, Sydney.

I suggest that our legislators might consider giving effect to one of the following alternatives:

From the expiration of one month from the date of the order calling for repairs, permit the tenant to withhold the full rent until the repairs have been carried out to the complete satisfaction of the proper authority.

Provide the authority with the means to have the repairs done at public cost, settlement with the owner to be made by proper processes as between him and the authority.

In either case, justice would be done to the tenant, who needs the support of the law; and also to the owner, who, in the second case, might plead circumstances that would induce the authority to bear part of the cost of repairs; as, for example, where the property was condemned, or, being leasehold, was of little or no value to the landlord.

Letters, F Shaw, Real Estate Institute of NSW. The postwar landlord and tenant legislation has resulted in the cessation of building for rental purposes and has rendered the ownership of this class of property an economic liability which is reacting to the detriment of thousands of tenants in the city and near city areas.

Only when the Government recognises the harm it is doing to the community as a whole and permits rental increase commensurate with the cost of living increases since 1939, will there be any improvement in the physical condition of property, not only in Redfern, but in every other district occupied by tenanted dwellings.

Letters, R S Osborne, Mosman. For 30 years I have owned three cottages at Mosman, and in that time have charged 27/6 a week rent for them.

Shortly after the war began, my three tenants began to take in boarders, and have continued to do so ever since. The result is that the tenants are living rent free while I am forced to pay higher rates to the council and big bills for painting and repairs.

The most bitter landlord-baiter will probably agree that Parliament never envisaged such an anomaly when it pegged rents in 1939.

WOMEN ON JURIES

Press release. The NSW Minister of Justice, Mr R Downing, announced that women would be eligible to serve on juries in Sydney and seven country districts. "People, both male and female, have been urging this since the end of the War. Parliament has passed legislation providing for this in 1947, and it has now been possible to implement this on a large scale.

"Women wishing to serve must apply to be included. After that, women will be included on the juror's list for next year. A lack of proper accommodation will prevent the making of appointments for other districts, but we hope to extend to other areas next year."

Comment. Women had gained a great deal of freedom and equality during WWII and were becoming aware that they had a long way to go. Some of them had been demanding access to the jury lists for years, and now they got that access, thought they were still free to apply or not apply, as they pleased. This would not have pleased the more fervent of the agitators because that wanted full equality with men, and they thought they could not have that unless, in this case, women were compelled to serve on the same basis as men.

A few Letter-writers had their say.

Letters, C Scrimgeour, United Associations of Women,. We congratulate Mr Downing on his finally proclaiming the bill to permit women to serve on juries. We hope that all eligible women will "want" to serve and thus go a step nearer towards becoming full-time, instead of part-time citizens.

We believe that legislation must go still further, by making service compulsory for women as for men, bringing us in line with women in many other countries, including England, where it is taken for granted that women recognise their responsibilities in this sphere.

From the perusal of trial reports and of Judges' comments regarding verdicts in several instances, it is becoming increasingly evident that the inclusion of women would improve the whole jury system.

Letters, Molly Gartner. I do not believe, like Caroline Scrimgeour that "legislation must go still further, by making (jury) service compulsory for women as for men."

Women in this country already carry a very heavy burden in their home tasks along with constant care of the young, the aged and the sick.

It is sufficiently difficult for the woman of average means to discharge these arduous duties satisfactorily, without the added burden of jury service, which, except in the possible field of child welfare, has been and can be done quite as well by the more leisured male.

It is admirable for women with spare time to devote themselves to these matters. Many women, however, work long hours and have little leisure.

These, no doubt, like myself, will strenuously resist any effort to introduce compulsory jury service.

Letters, Caroline Scrimgeour, United Assns. Of Women.   In reaffirming our belief that jury service should be equally compulsory for men and women, we would remind Molly Gartner that there would not necessarily be greater hardship for women than for men.

Exemptions for men from jury service are very liberal and it would follow they would be equally so for women. The main reason for woman's greater "burden" is her lack of representation in places which could lighten that burden. So long as she accepts inferior status, in law and in traditional habit, her problems will continue to be overlooked or neglected.

ATOM BOMB AT MONTE BELLO

The nation awoke on October 4th to the news that the Brits (and Oz) had successfully exploded an atom bomb on Monte Bello Islands, off the north west coast of Australia. We were told that test had been successful, though what that meant was not explained. We also learned that the Queen and Winston Churchill had been informed, that three Oz observers had been present, and that naval personnel had viewed the episode on TV from below deck.

As to the explosion itself, we were treated to the reports that said there had been a bright flash followed by a red glow, a low rumble was heard from miles away, and that smoke had risen to 10,000 feet. In the township of Onslow, on the mainland coast, it was reported breathlessly that cups rattled on tables, doors swung on their hinges, and a horse being saddled shied and bolted across a half-acre paddock. Drinkers in the Beadon Hotel, the only one in town, were startled by the news that the hotel had only three more crates of beer in stock. This dampened the party that was celebrating the "success". A few days later, Adelaide said that radio active rain fell harmlessly there, and two more days later Melbourne reported similarly.

Comment. You can see that I was not much impressed by all this. The newspapers used their hush-hush tones to imply that all of this was very important, even historic. But it wasn't. America and Russia had been having great fun destroying islands and deserts for a few years now, and mushroom clouds were a dime a dozen. The newspapers, reflecting the official political line, sought to convince readers that the fact that Australia was involved a little at the margins made this into a big deal.

The Brits probably achieved what they set out to do. It seems to me that they wanted to prove to themselves that they could fire a bomb, and now they were **sure** that they could. Of equal importance was that it was now obvious to the Americans that Britain had all the basic know-how, and that their monopoly in this area had gone. This might influence them to share with the Brits their more advanced knowledge.

Australia gained little from all this, I believe. We **still** did not go on to develop our own bomb, and we have not developed a nuclear industry, nor have we commissioned nuclear power stations. As to those atomic secrets, by now there were many spies active in many nations that were trading them, and also many scientists who were moving about with sufficient freedom to make sure that information was shared on an increasingly common basis.

Britain's tests, with and without Australian help, continued until 1958. In Britain, over 1,000 British soldiers, who witnessed Monte Bello, mounted a class-action suit against the Government in 2009, claiming damage to their health from bomb-induced cancer and other maladies. Governments, worldwide, have been deliberately slow to acknowledge any such impairments to health, and, for example, the Brits have spent decades avoiding court cases on the issue.

NEWS AND VIEWS

Car-minders. In 1952, suppose you parked your car in the city of Casablanca. In the minds of Australians, it was a place of intrigue and romance, where gallantry and true love both flourished eternally. But, as you would find out as you left your car, it was also a city where car minders did their own bit of flourishing. These gentlemen, dirtier and dressed even worse that Humphrey Bogart, would have descended on you, and demanded that they be commissioned to guard your car, and that you pay for the privilege. As it turned out, if you did not accede to their requests, you would run the risk that somehow, in your absence, your car would suffer considerable damage, and may even be undrivable. The men who thus offered their guardianship services were known as car minders, and they could be found in most cities of Europe and North Africa.

By 1952, they had migrated to Australia, and appeared in the streets of our bigger cities, waiting anxiously to benefit society with their protective expertise. Strangely, though, not everyone welcomed them. A *SMH* Editorial complained about them and argued that the motorist nowadays pays Customs tax, sales tax, petrol tax, Bridge tolls, fees, fines, and every other sort of impost that official ingenuity can devise. And then, when he brings his car to the city, a man in a grubby white coat holds out his hand and demands more. The article pointed out that most minders collected their money and just went home. It said that motorists would not mind paying if any real service was provided, but argued that this was not the case. And concluded that the car-minding racket is a nuisance, and an imposition, and at worst a menace.

But, argues Alderman Thompson below, perhaps minders could be regulated to provide a worthwhile service.

Letters, (Ald) Albert Thompson. Whilst all motorists will agree with your leader of October 8, "The Pettiest of Petty Rackets," the impression I have gained in conversation with many car owners is that they feel it is better to have some protection of an unattended car than no protection at all in this period of **daily car theft** and interference.

It is cheaper in the long run to pay the impost than to have your car stolen or damaged.

I believe the only way to deal immediately with the situation is **to license car minders under proper supervision of the Police Traffic Department**, making the department responsible for the character and conduct of car minders, and to set a small fee for the service.

The peace of mind and security obtained would make it worthwhile to the average motorist and it would give employment to many deserving men past the age of normal employment but vigorous enough to do the job.

Comment. By 1960, car minders were well and truly on their way out. It turned out that local Councils saw the light and the cash cow, and decided to impose their own form of car-minding on the citizenry. That is, they started to introduce **parking meters**, so that those meters would milk the public and provide exactly the same level of protection as the car-minders had. And even more profitable, someone thought up the **idea of parking police** to extract as much money as possible. The car-minders could not compete, so that, like so many other noble professions today, the intricacies of car-minding have now been pushed onto the scrap-heap of history.

The solution to parking problems in cities. The writer below had the solution to over-crowding in city parking.

Letters, Jenny Tenukest. Here is a simple solution to the city parking deadlock. It will allow each vehicle to park on alternate days, and is regulated by the last numeral on the registration plate and the date of the month. Thus, if "A's" car number is GV210 and "B's" car number is GV211, for example, then "A" can park on all even dates while "B" can park only on odd days. This system would reduce city parking by half and would be fair to all.

Comment. It seems to me there is a flaw in her proposal, but I can't for the life of me put my finger on it. Perhaps you can.

NOVEMBER: KOREA YET AGAIN

Once again, I bring the sad news that the Korean War was still going on. Right now, the land battles were getting more ferocious, with the various armies fighting over several "hills" and proclaiming victories when they won one, or won it back. Still, the battle-front was about static, and only the numbers of dead and maimed changed. Those numbers never seemed to go down.

The main obstacle to peace seemed to be all of those prisoners-of-war. Now totalling well over 100,000 on both sides, the question was still whether, if released, they wanted to go home to where their families and friends were, to where they would have a job and housing, and to where they were heroes. Or did they want to go to a foreign country where they would have none of these, and be a pariah. The warring parties, especially America, thinking in terms of propaganda, still hoped that lots of Reds would opt to change sides and were holding out for some affirmation of that.

Somehow, India had gotten into the act in the last month. It was a neutral country, and supposedly could act as a mediator, nicely balanced between Capitalist and Communist worlds. But after a lot of messing about on all sides, by the end of November nothing had been decided, and from what you could read, it was all the fault of the other parties. **They** really were the worst of baddies.

IndoChina. The Reds in IndoChina (Vietnam, Cambodia, and Laos) were now on the march, and had earned the dubious title of "insurgents" in our local press. They were receiving military support from China, and wanted to take over their countries. They were currently harassing the French colonial forces, and if you had to make a bet, you might say the French will not have the stamina to defend their interests there for too long.

That is a story for later years, but I point out that the basis for the famous Vietnam War of 1966 was being laid now.

TWO BIG RACES ON THE SAME DAY

The Americans are jealous of our Melbourne Cup, and every two years hold their national elections on the first Tuesday in November. This, of course, is the same day as we hold the Melbourne Cup, and their idea is simply to steal the limelight from us on the grandest day of our national calendar. But try as they might, they always come in second in the PR race. This year, the new President Eisenhower had a landslide victory with only a little hubbub here in Oz.

On the other hand, the Cup once again stopped this nation, everyone had a bet or was in a sweep, half the men came home tiddly, and the nation happily felt the grand day was another success. For the record, let me say that this year, the Cup was won by a horse. Its name escapes me, but it's too late to have a bet, anyway. Not that you could in those days, because it was illegal to bet on a horse unless you were at a race track. So you couldn't possibly have had a bet - could you!!?

Many of our schools across the nation had a new toy to play with. **Public address systems had been installed,** and so it was possible to broadcast important messages right into the classrooms. What could be more important than the Melbourne Cup? Nothing of course, so many schools did just that. Not everyone agreed that this was a good thing.

Letters, A Langdon, Church of England Diocese of Sydney. The item which headed your Column 8 of November 5 gives cause for alarm and demands some action to prevent a repetition of the use of the loud-speaker system in schools for the broadcast of the Melbourne Cup – a purpose for which they were certainly not installed, either by the Education Department or by Parents and Citizens' Associations.

Is not the gambling spirit of this country fostered enough already without actively and officially encouraging children's interest in the Cup under the guise of a "current events" lesson? Since when has the Melbourne Cup been included in the Education Department's syllabus for current events, Australian history or anything else?

Many of your readers will probably be inclined to retort that to listen to the Cup does not mean one is gambling. May I reply in advance by asking how many people who take an active interest in the cup do so solely because of their earnest desire to keep abreast of "current events"?

The schools' official educational imprimatur on the Cup is certainly doing nothing to discourage the gambling spirit (a responsibility the school has to the community). The next thing will be that the school is using its loud-speakers to broadcast the results of the present unofficial school sweeps, which are yet another indication of the growth of the gambling spirit in the younger generation.

Why should children from Christian homes who have had to take their stand for Christ in the school against the gambling menace on Cup day, then be forced to sit and listen to the Cup as part of their school curriculum?

Are we not entitled to know whether this abuse of school equipment and time has been introduced with the knowledge and approval of the Minister for Education?

Letters, W Rugendyke, Minister of Church of Christ.
If this "current events" broadcast was a real step in education and more than a crude sham, then we should expect that teachers would point out the evils of gambling.

It is sincerely to be hoped that the education authorities will regard very seriously this breach of moral discipline.

Letters, Pedagogue. As a teacher in a school under the control of the Education Department, I resent the assumption by your correspondents of November 6 that the use of loud-speaker systems to broadcast the Cup necessarily occurred in Departmental schools.

Although **I have never heard of such a thing being done in our public schools**, I know of at least one exclusive boarding school, under the control of a Church, which has never frowned on gambling and where official notice is or was taken of the Melbourne Cup. As well, some of **the girls** were assembled to hear the broadcast!

The attitude taken by previous correspondents towards public schools is becoming more common today, viz that they are hotbeds of godlessness.

Letters, R Gollan. For long it has been an accepted educational principle that schools do their best to equip the youngster to take his place in society. This is an impossibility unless both students and public feel that some measure of relationship exists between the school and the tempo of the world around it.

We do not suggest in consequence that gambling be encouraged in schools. We do feel, however, that it is ridiculous for the school to deny the nation-wide interest in the Cup which in reality is no longer a mere race but a national event in itself.

The Rev Mr Langdon has inferred that only those children who "take their stand...against gambling" are

Christians.   Are then the thousands of penny-sweep fans to be classified pagan?   Far from children being "forced to sit and listen to the Cup," a torrent of protest followed the announcement that they could not listen in our school.   In the face of such interest and feeling, has anyone the right arbitrarily to decree "Thou shalt not"?

CONTROL OF TV

TV had been introduced into Britain and the US by the late 1930's, and its growth over the next decade had been steady and substantial.   Australia, maintaining its not-so-silly reputation for being late-adopters, lagged a long way behind in its introduction here.   In fact, it came to us only in 1956, in time for our hosting of the Olympics in Melbourne.

So the planning in 1952 was at its early stages. We of course wanted to use the failures and success in Britain and the US to teach us lessons. But these two countries had come at it from different angles.   Britain had a very widely respected BBC radio service, and it set up its TV with the same model in place.   That is, there was **no commercial TV at all**. Just a number of different BBC channels.   America, on the other hand, had **all commercial telecasters**, and no government-backed channels.

The question here became which of these two models should we follow?   Or, perhaps, we should merge the two somehow?   In any case, given the fact that we had a small population, and relatively few big corporations that would advertise, could we have commercial stations in the country areas with even fewer large corporations to foot the bill? Tough questions.

The *SMH*, in a November 26th Editorial, opted for a dual system. It said that the ABC and commercials interests should be allowed to compete on equal terms. It also said that, on the one hand, Australians should be protected from the worst abuses of commercial broadcasting, as seen in America. On the other hand, it should avoid setting up a monopoly that might be used by an unscrupulous government for its own ends. Hence, the dual system.

Letters, D Stewart, WEA of NSW. The Council of the Workers' Educational Association has suggested to the Government that a Commission be set up to hear evidence and present a report before any decision is reached with regard to the development of television in Australia.

Criticism of television services in other countries emphasises the dangers which may follow lack of adequate care to ensure high-standard programmes.

Undoubtedly, children are strongly affected by television, and it must in a very short time affect the cultural standards of the whole community.

We do not presume to say what is the best form of organisation for television, but we believe the matter is so important as to warrant the fullest inquiry while there is yet time.

Letters, William Sterling. To throw the initial development of television directly into the hands of commercial sponsors would be dangerous.

The Government, through the ABC, should at least direct the standards of presentation. This might be done through the Broadcasting Control Board.

American TV, established as a purely commercial venture, has shown that for the first few years the initial financial outlay was fantastically expensive and entertainment standards, in many instances, were, and are still, deplorable.

Letters, M Kennett, NSW Teachers' Federation. The executive of the New South Wales Teachers' Federation is opposed to amendment of the Broadcasting Act so as to permit the establishment of commercial television.

Because of the harmful effects commercial television has had on American children, as revealed in reports from US educational authorities, our executive wishes to restate its policy, and that of the **Australian Teachers' Federation Conference** of 1951, that **television should be the sole preserve of the Government.**

Letters, J B Yorke. Your editorial advocating a dual system of national and commercial television ignores the point that, by its very nature, television is essentially monopolistic. **Outside of Sydney and Melbourne it is unlikely that any city would be able to support more than one station.**

The danger, suggested by your article, that an unscrupulous Government might use a monopoly for its own ends seems rather illusory when we consider the tradition of impartial service established by the ABC and the BBC.

The fantastic cost of sponsoring commercial television networks in the USA has meant that fewer than 200 corporations can afford to use this service. In Australia it would not be unreasonable to assume that fewer than 20 business undertakings could sponsor a network programme.

Free enterprisers who are anxious that commercial TV be established in Australia might have second thoughts when it is realised that as an advertising medium it would be the exclusive preserve of a handful of our largest companies.

Is it not better that an industry, which is inherently monopolistic, should be run as a national undertaking instead of being left to commercial interests?

Letters, H Smith, Associated TV.   Mr Kennett, speaking for the NSW Teachers' Federation, has dealt only with the negative possibilities of television.

Perhaps he has not read the opinions of leading American educational authorities who claim that "TV is the finest educational instrument ever invented." He fears commercial television, but does not understand that the spread of population and the long distances between centres would make the operation of television in Australia on other than a commercial basis, hopeless.

In any case, his fears of the "harmful effects" on children are exaggerated.   Every modern development brings with it liabilities, but we do not ban motor transport because of the harmful effect of road accidents.

Television, on a scale made possible by commercial support, may be used to effectively overcome obstacles such as shortages in teaching staffs and accommodation, if the authorities will prove themselves capable of using the new medium.

Comment   As you know, Oz did go for the dual model, though over the next year, the argument about this grew more severe. Country centres **now** seem to be able to afford two commercial stations, and a local ABC relay. So all in all, maybe we did get the best of both worlds, and maybe it was to our advantage to have dawdled a bit in setting it all up.

NAMING FLOWERS IS KIDS STUFF

Letters, S Craddock. Mr "Paddy" Pallin, of Sydney, a well-known bush-walker and honorary wildflower ranger, recently suggested that such wildflowers as Isotoma fluviatalis, Hymenosporum flavum and Phebalium dentatum should be give common names.

In passing, he mentioned black-eyed Susan, the waratah and drumstick which, had it not been for someone's facile naming, might still be known only as Tetratheca ericifolia, Telopea speciosissima and Ispopogon anethifolius.

Impressed by Mr Pallin's agreeable suggestion, we called to ask whether he had any particular common names in mind, but we drew a rather surprising blank.

"Only a child or a poet can name a flower," he said with what sounded like a poetical turn of phrase. "And I am neither. My only constructive suggestion is that, if you could familiarise people with our native flowers, more suitable names would soon evolve. You have to know a person well before you give him a nick-name, don't you?

In England, every wildflower has it own name – Ladies' Bed Straw, Arch Angels and Eglantine."

Mr Pallin's desire for more vernacular names may not strike a chord of response in some scientific circles. There have, in the past, been many complaints about misunderstandings due to popular nomenclature of both our flora and fauna. For instance, is a Mountain devil a lizard or a plant? It is both.

Letters, D Watts. While everyone would wish with Mr Souter and Mr Pallin that more Australian flowers had common names, it is to be hoped that poets will not leave invention to children, for the horrid truth is **that children are more belly than soul.**

In Western Australia there is a delicate, pale, green cup brimming with tiny, cream stars. The children call it "Bread-and-cheese." There are little, pink bells that hang in graceful sprays which childish fancy has named "Salt-and-pepper." There is a large purple iris that might be expected to catch a child's eye; but the children see only the brown spathe from which the flowers come, and call it "Fishes." There is a lovely, large pea-flower of the richest orange colour veined with soft, warm brown. The little children call it "Eggs-and-bacon."

Even when their minds wander away from things to eat they do not do much better. There are flowers that are spread over the ground like miniature suns fallen out of light, but these make less appeal to the child than does the somewhat grotesque fruit that comes after. They call the shining wonder, "Pig face." There is a grass that comes to a beautifully made catkin-like head. Last month it bubbled in breathtaking acres of green foam. The little fiends call this exquisite thing – I hate to write it – "Blowfly grass."

From internal evidence I should say that it was the poets among the country-folk, and not the children, who named the English flowers so sweetly – "Love-in-a-mist," "Day's eyes,", "Pan's eyes," and "Forget-me-nots."

GOD'S LOVABLE LITTLE CREATURES

News from our special fly reporter.

Swarms of small flies pestered residents of coastal suburbs yesterday. Few people stayed long on the beaches because of the flies. Surf officials at Bondi, North Bondi, Manly, Deewhy, and Maroubra said that the insects – which they described as the "clinging type" – were thick at the beaches. "It is hopeless to try and sun-bathe or relax on the sands," a Manly lifesaver said.

The Manly chief health inspector, Mr C Membrey, warned residents to keep all food covered because the flies were a possible menace to health. Mr Membrey said he believed that the flies were blown from below Sutherland by Saturday night's southerly gale.

Comment. This article was front-page news on the *SMH*.

Now from our roving ant-man-on-the-spot.

Letters, A J Hemmons. Thirty years' residence in Burma, an ant-infested country, where bed and kitchen furniture had to be kept standing in pots of kerosene and water, taught me that the only way to get rid of ants is to go after them. The process of attrition does the trick, with patience.

No small ants, such as the Argentine variety, stand up to a spray of kerosene with a good dash of petrol in it. An ordinary fly-spraying pump will do.

Chlordane may be all that is claimed for it – but no kind of food poison will do so much mass destruction as the kero spray, and the general habit of the ant tribe lends itself to mass destruction. Moreover, the kero spray pump is cheap and within the reach of everybody.

The only occasion I know of when poison cleared my entire house of ants was when, during my absence, they found my medicine cupboard and completely cleaned up a bottle of chlorodyne and about 30 tabloids of bismuth subsantonate. This was in Mandalay. We never had another ant in the place.

Not to be outdone, our Bogong reporter gets into the act.

News item. Bogong moths, in minor plague numbers, are making their seasonal appearance yesterday in the suburbs, from Hornsby to Roseville.

Mr Musgrave, chief entomologist at the Australian Museum, said the Bogong moth was essentially an outdoor moth, but for the last fortnight people living in the northern suburbs and other parts of Sydney had found them in their houses. It was not uncommon to find the moths between blankets in a bed.

"In the hot weather you frequently find them on the summits of hills," he said. "In the old days aborigines used to congregate on the moths clustered as thick as bees in rock crevices. They would burn the wings and scales from the moths, fill bags with them, and pound them into a paste which was considered a delicacy."

There were minor plagues of the moths in Sydney every few years. In 1867 the moths disrupted a service in St. Thomas's Church, North Sydney. They were so thick on the church windows that they blacked out the light.

This is Australia, so of course there has to be a contribution from our **specialist snake expert**.

Letters, Tim Cloke. A man was bitten by a snake at the Outdoor Show in the Sydney Town Hall last week. This is of interest to all snake-lovers. Your report states that the snake struck the victim's arm after moving inside his sleeve almost to his elbow. I do not doubt this, but it again raises the old question: Do snakes strike in the dark? Ordinarily, in my opinion, the answer is: no.

It was also reported that the victim "thought he had tamed" the snake. My experience is that "taming" cannot be applied to snakes. A snake may be "broken to handle" by one person, yet resent handling by another. Yet I am surprised that an even partially broken-to-handle snake should strike from inside the handler's sleeve. The handler must surely have attempted forcibly to pull the snake back.

I have studied the methods of snakeologists in all parts of the world and do not hesitate to say that the Australian snakeologist can hold his own with any. I would specially commend the suction-cup method of extracting venom, as used by the victim of the Town Hall incident. If widely adopted it would greatly reduce the risk of ill-effects.

And finally, words of wisdom from **our whaling ace**.

Letters, Melville Scott (ex-Whaler). Reference in *The Sunday Herald* to the closing of the surf at Mona Vale on Saturday because a school of sharks "attacked a whale" off the beach, prompts me to point out that each year at this time several species of whales are seen in these latitudes, travelling south.

Their purpose inshore is to rid themselves of sea-lice and other parasites by rubbing against rocks and sandy ocean beds. Large schools of fish attend the big mammals, feeding on the offal and generally assisting in the delousing.

It is these fish that the sharks - particularly the thresher – attack by threshing with their tails and striking the water with a force that stuns a number of the fish, which they then devour. The also leap and strike the water with the same stunning effect which, at a distance, might give the impression that they were attacking the whale, but this is not possible.

The only place on the huge body of a whale that would offer the sharks' jaws a grip is that region adjoining the tail known as the "small," and here the attacker would be quickly dispatched with one mighty blow from the flailing extremity.

The sperm whale, mentioned in your report, is the least vulnerable of all. Besides being more voracious than other species, it is a true "denizen of the deep," and at threat of danger dives many fathoms below, where enemies cannot follow.

NEWS AND VIEWS

November 17th. Australian **Jimmy Carruthers** won the World Bantamweight Boxing title from South African Vic Toweel, by knocking him out in the first round of their bout. Carruthers was the first Australian ever to win a World Title. Toweel did not land a single punch. The fight lasted only two minutes, and 19 seconds.

November 20th. The Sydney Water Board said today that 500,000 persons in Sydney were waiting for sewerage. Most readers will remember what that means. All those trips up the garden path to the dunny, built as close as possible to the neighbour's back yard, at all times of the day and night, in all types of weather. Fun.

November 22nd. Government estimated that in Sydney alone 30,000 **owner-builders** were doing their own thing. This was mainly because it was so hard to get a bank loan, and because it was much easier to build a garage on the back of a block, and live in it, and then build your house in small stages as you accumulated the finance.

DECEMBER: 10 HIT SONGS:

All Of Me	Johnnie Ray
Heart And Soul	Four Aces
Here In my Heart	Al Martino
High Noon	Frankie Lane
I Saw Mummy Kissing Santa	Jimmy Boyd
A Kiss to Build A Dream On	Louis Armstrong
Unforgettable	Nat King Cole
Walkin' My Baby Back Home	Guy Mitchell
Winter Wonderland	Perry Como
When I Fall in Love	Doris Day

10 MOVIES RELEASED

Affair in Trinadad	Rita Hayworth
The Bad and the Beautiful	Turner, Mitchum
High Noon	Gary Cooper
Limelight	Charlie Chaplin
My Cousin Rachael	de Haviland
Pat and Mike	Tracy, Hepburn
Road to Bali	Hope, Crosby
Singin' In the Rain	Kelly, Reynolds
The Stooges	Martin, Lewis
Bud, Lou meet Captain Kidd	Bud and Lou

ACADEMY AWARDS:

Best Actor: Gary Cooper (High Noon)
Best Actress: Shirley Booth (Come Back, Little Sheba)

IS IT CHRISTMAS OR XMAS?

Every year, at about this time, for as long as I can remember, Oz society has decided that it will have a grand festival towards the end of December. They called it Christmas. It seems that there was once an obvious reason for this many years ago, but that now, with the passage of time, the reason is becoming obscure, and many people are finding **that** quite objectionable.

Apparently, in the dim distant days, the Christian Churches were very much at the centre of the occasion, and people used to flock to the churches to celebrate their big day with reverence. But by 1952, the Churches were suffering a decline in attendance and influence, and were fighting stoutly to arrest the trend. For example, Catholic priests were recently bemoaning the fact that the number of Requiem Masses for the dead had fallen sharply, and Protestant clergy were disturbed as they saw that parishioners were coming to Church nowadays only on festive occasions, and not regularly every Sunday. Both sets of clergy saw that society was getting more and more worldly and materialistic and, **fighting back,** were striving to put Christ back as the focus of our daily life.

So with the celebration of Christmas approaching, it was not at all surprising to see Letters published that argued for strengthening the religious connotations of the season.

Letters, R I R. More than ever this year, there is a dearth of gift cards that have any reference to the true meaning of Christmas. There are comic card, cards featuring animals and birds, and plenty of cards depicting flowers and gardens, but cards that have any reference to the Nativity are hard to find and of poor quality.

Surely a card depicting the watchful shepherds with a caption such as "Peace on earth, goodwill to men" is more in keeping with the spirit of Christmas than a performing dog or a basket of flowers, and would have a greater appeal for children.

Letters, J F K. The public refuses to buy Christmas cards of a religious character.

Fashions change in all merchandise, and though in mid-Victorian days such cards were in constant demand, they are now unpopular. It is exactly the same with children's religious books. Such works as "Tip Lewis and his Lamp" sold in their thousands 50 years ago, but nowadays a gift of this nature to children on Christmas morning would prompt them to yawn in one's face. This may be very sad, but the retailer must meet public demand.

Letters, E A Jackson. Something should be done to offset the pagan spirit that is changing Christmas to "Xmas" and a holy day into a mere holiday.

Holiday ornaments, carols, etc., are not out of order, provided they do not add up to a top-heavy stress upon Christmas as a mere holiday. "Jingle Bells" should not drown out "Adeste Fideles" and "Silent Night."

Any campaign to "salvage Christmas for Christ" should be **focalised** in the mind and heart. It is not inappropriate to read Dickens' "Christmas Carols," but it is much more to the point to read and ponder the gospel accounts of the advent of the Christ Child as recorded in the New Testament. Why not boycott cards that feature meaningless snow-bound homesteads, candles, and even dogs? A holy Christmas is certain to be a happy Christmas.

Letters, WORRIED MOTHER. Many parents must be as worried as I am over promises made to children by Santa Claus in some city stores.

There was a time when Santas were careful not to compromise parents by promising something expensive, but this unwritten rule seems to have been abandoned. Last week my little boy visited Santa, and because he was wearing a cowboy jumper, Santa led the conversation to cowboys and camping and then promised him a play-tent.

We are now in a quandary. We cannot afford a play-tent, yet without ruining the child's faith in Santa, cannot convince him that the gift will not materialise. He says "it will come – Santa told me himself; I didn't even ask for it."

That, sir, is hardly cricket.

THE TV DEBATE RAGES ON

The debate on the merits of various proposals matured. The Australian Chapter of the World Council of Churches started the ball rolling in December by urging that a committee of enquiry should be set up, to study all aspects of TV. Perhaps even a Royal Commission would be required.

Mr Anthony, the Post Master General, responded by talking generally about people who wanted such enquiries being motivated by the desire to delay its introduction. He went on to placate some criticism by praising the British system which allowed TV for only a couple of hours in the mornings, then a few hours in the afternoon for children, and finally three hours for evening programmes.

The Director of the NSW Chamber of Commerce was more forthright. "The present criticism and fear of TV comes from **the universal human characteristic to oppose anything**

new. Those who criticised and **opposed the radio receiver** chose exactly the same arguments as the opponents of TV today. Australia weathered the innovation of radio and came out of it a better informed and entertained nation despite the weakness and stupidity of a fair proportion of programmes. The dangers, of allowing TV to be controlled by a committee of idealists, is that the public will only be given what the idealists believe it should be given, and it is unlikely the public and the idealists will see eye to eye on this."

An article in the *SMH* quoted three prominent Americans who had spoken out against TV. Justice Felix Frankfurter, of the Supreme Court, said it was a new barbarism, parading as scientific progress. Dr Hooton, of Harvard, predicted that man will debase himself to the status of a well-behaved domestic animal. A child psychologist, Dr Wortham, insisted that TV gives children the point of view which confuses violence with strength, low necklines with feminine ideal, and criminals with police. The article went on to say that many august institutions had found that TV was more beneficial than damaging, but it was still clearly a matter of debate.

These statements prompted a further flood of Letters. Below, I enclose a fair sample.

Letters, A E Mander. It is good to see the "Herald" standing firm amid the clamour of interested parties trying to stampede the Government into throwing television open to those whose sole consideration would be, "How can we exploit this invention for our own financial gain?"

Here is a new force coming into the life of mankind, and one which must possess immense potentialities for either evil or good. It will have the power of either stimulating or deadening the minds of millions; of forming people's tastes and standards of beauty; even more important, of guiding millions of people in the sort of behaviour they will come to regard as admirable, to be emulated. Television may turn out to be the most potent of all influences in determining "what sort of people" the next generation will be.

It is disappointing to see Dr Evatt supporting the Minister in advocating a headlong rush into commercialised television. One cannot help noting the more responsible nature of the stand taken, not only by the "Herald", but also by Mr Calwell, MP, and the Churches. This is not primarily an economic question or even a political one; it is a moral question, a question as to what will be best for the well being of the people of Australia.

Letters, Leicester Webb, Australian National University. One aspect of the television problem has so far received too little attention – the impact of television on politics.

It may or may not be true that private interests can be relied on to uphold "the canons of good taste." But it is certainly not true that the question of the political use to be made of television can be left to the decision of private interests.

On American experience it can be said that television is potentially the most powerful instrument of political propaganda yet devised and that it will inevitably strengthen influences already making for the centralisation of political power. It would surely be wise not to put this instrument in the hands of private interests until we have made up our minds what safeguards are necessary in the interests of democratic government.

There is still doubt and confusion over the proper safeguards for ordinary political broadcasting in Australia. The present position is, to say the least, unsatisfactory; and it will become much more unsatisfactory with the added complication of television.

I would add that it is quite as dangerous to leave this problem to the two main political parties to solve as it is to leave it to private interests.

Letters, T H Upton. There is one phase of the matter which seems to have escaped public attention but which is of pre-eminent importance at this stage to Australia's development.

That is, that whatever human effort and money is put into this activity will not be available for other use.

We are far behind in providing all the fundamental public needs – houses, hospitals, schools, water supply and conservation, transport, sewerage, and power.

Yet apparently we are considering embarking upon a new activity, much less needed than any of these, and devoted primarily to entertainment.

Surely we need the more fundamental things first and should be devoting our financial and physical resources to them rather than considering the luxury of television until at least the former are in measurable sight of being provided?

Letters, Woodstock. Surely the Government is aware of the likely economic impact on Australian industry if television falls into the hungry maw of commercial interests.

The cost of any article necessarily includes its proportion of all overhead charges, including advertising. It is not unnatural to assume that television advertised products will become more expensive.

Do we want this trend in Australia at a time of inflation?

ANOTHER COMMENT ON BROKEN HILL

Broken Hill was still regarded round Australia as the City of the Wild West. Plenty of grog at all hours, two-up rings, girls, fights, and perhaps fame and fortune from the mines – somehow. It was now reported in the Press that over Christmas **a trainload of revellers from Sydney** was planning to visit the fair city, and enjoy the so-called delights.

There were of course large cries of indignation against this. But this Letter spoke up for the City, if not for the aspirations of the would-be revelers.

Letters, E C Savage, Broken Hill. There has been so much commotion about the Broken Hill privilege that I fear to add to it, but would like to say this:

I am an Englishman who has made Australia his home. I have memories of pleasant evenings spent in some quiet English country pub, where beer was recognised as one of the good things of life, to be enjoyed and savoured and not wallowed in – where in quiet surroundings and pleasant society one could enjoy an evening pint.

To me, coming to this young and very lively land, the second most annoying thing was the incredible asininity of regulations concerning licensing, which were surely designed to encourage drunkenness and to debase a social custom to a standing disgrace. During my stay in Sydney earlier this year, I took, perhaps, four or five glasses in seven weeks. The prospect of entering into the "swill," as I believe it is called, was just too uncivilised.

Here at Broken Hill the situation is much improved. It is possible to enjoy a drink, not merely to swallow it. Of course, the written law of the State is flouted; but let us hope that the present judicial examination of customs overseas will lead to the amendment of the present law and the rescue of an old custom from its present degradation.

Perhaps, as an ancillary movement to this renaissance, an attempt should be made to educate "the masses" in the proper appreciation, and use of what is, after all, one of God's gifts. I suggest that Chesterton's essay on "Wine, when it is red" should be a compulsory study in the English syllabus in the secondary stage of our schools.

HOUSING SHORTAGES

A nationwide housing shortage was bugging all of the newly-wed returned servicemen and their new brides and babies. Citizens were free to build or buy their own home, but a shortage of bank finance meant that only those with a big deposit and a good job could get a house that way. So the various **States** came up with schemes whereby **they** built large numbers of houses on estates, and then sold them off to applicants. Of course, the number of houses thus built was a lot smaller than the number of applicants, so some mechanism was needed to pick the lucky people who got them. In NSW, the Housing Commission, which owned the new houses, decided to do this by lottery.

This meant that thousands of young couples put their names in a hat, and every now and then a number of them would be selected and advised that they were eligible to buy a government-built house on these estates. For the lucky ones, this worked out well But for the majority, those who missed out in ballot after ballot, it was a torturous waiting period with no certainty that they would **ever** be selected.

There was a great deal of criticism of this scheme, and similar ones in other States. I cannot hope to cover all of this here, so all I have done is provide three letters to give you an idea of some of the issues that this difficult situation engendered.

Letters, Eric Willis, MLA for Earlwood. I have read with some misgivings the news of two recent ballots for Housing Commission homes conducted by the Minister for Housing, Mr Clive Evatt.

It will be recalled that in the three months immediately prior to the State election of 1950 (a comparable time with the present), Mr Evatt conducted ballots for 75 single bedroom, 350 two-bedroom, and 300 three-bedroom homes. These houses, it later turned out, were not completed and, indeed, some had not even been begun. In a number of cases successful applicants had to wait 12 months before receiving the homes they had won.

Letters, Clive Evatt, Minister for Housing. Mr E Willis displays lamentable ignorance of Housing Commission procedure in the allocation of homes.

Ballots are held by the Housing Commission not in respect of particular dwellings or projects, but in advance of accommodation becoming available in the different categories. This procedure has been adopted so that there will always be a number of successful ballotees with whom tenancy agreements can be made immediately suitable dwellings are available for letting.

The waiting period is seldom protracted, but there must, of necessity, be some gap between success at ballot and the commencement of tenancy as the Commission conducts a careful post-ballot investigation to see whether the ballotee's circumstance have undergone any change since he first applied. Then again, there are other incidental delays – completion of tenancy agreements, removal of furniture, etc. Any lengthy interval is usually due to non-acceptance of the allocated dwelling by the successful ballotee.

I was not Minister for Housing after the 1950 elections, but I am informed by Commission officers that any delays in 1950 allocations were due to the failure of successful ballotees to accept the dwellings originally allotted to them because of personal considerations, such as distance from place of employment, transport facilities, and so forth.

Records establish that at the period referred to in Mr Willis's letter, there were no fewer than 3,450 dwellings under construction in the metropolitan area, many of them practically completed, and that there were ample dwellings in a virtually finished state to meet the requirements of ballots to which he refers.

Those successful in current ballots have my assurance that there are ample homes on the verge of completion to enable allocations on the completion of the usual post-ballot investigations.

Letters, Eric Willis, MLA for Earlwood. The Minister for Housing, Mr C Evatt, in his letter of December 24, attacked my "lamentable ignorance of Housing Commission procedure," but evaded the real issue which I raised.

I have not questioned the Housing Commission's procedure; I question only Mr Evatt's election tactics.

Can he deny that he rushed through ballots for three-bedroom houses in the six weeks prior to the 1950 State elections, and then no further ballots were held for such houses for another 18 months? Can he deny that a number of successful applicants in ballots held just before this election were compelled to wait from six to 12 months for their homes, even though there had been no change whatever in their housing circumstances?

SUMMING UP 1952

1952 was a very mixed year. It certainly had its fair share of problems, many more than last year. The main one was the economy. This year it was flat and getting flatter. Arthur Fadden, the Federal Treasurer, came out in December and told an incredulous nation that things were pretty good, and that next year we would certainly approach the El Dorado that was always promised, for **next** year. **Yeah, right, thanks Arthur.**

Much of the real problem with our economy sprang from the fact that our politicians were all obsessed, nearly all the time, with ridiculous point-scoring against other politicians from their own Party and others. The idea of developing national policies on a grand scale to advance the economy was too hard amid the abounding pettiness. So **what's new**, I hear you ask, and what has changed? My answer is "**nothing**", and I don't suppose it ever will. But 1952 seemed to be one of those years when almost no policies of significance ruffled the Parliamentary waters, and as I look back over it, I shake my head at the opportunities lost.

There was just one major policy initiative that impressed me. But, first, at the end of every book, **I indulge myself**, get off the fence as an author, and talk freely about one small matter of interest to me. In this case, it is **education**, but **I will digress** to a few places before I make my point.

The most outstanding event in 1952 to millions of sports-lovers was the victory of Jimmy Carruthers in gaining the World Title. Apart from the jingoistic pride, it validated a creed that was held by many of **our so-called and self-confessed no-hopers in the population.** That was, that **there were three ways out of poverty. One** was to win a lottery. The **second** was to get a greyhound dog that turned out to be a champion. The **third** was to become a champion fighter. That was what Carruthers had become. Thousands of young men now dreamed of getting fame and fortune by the same route.

Now, still digressing, but back to politics. The Federal Government in 1951 approved a new scheme that gave a few thousand University Commonwealth **scholarships** to students. These carried with them the payment of fees and a pittance that a moderate student could live on. What this meant was that, for years from 1952, a few thousand young people **each year**, who previously had no hope of going to university, could now enter those august places of learning. **This added a fourth strategy of climbing from poverty.** It meant that sensible students could study their way out, without having their head punched in or walking themselves as thin as a greyhound.

So, **now back on track**, after all my earlier criticism of the Federal Government for lack of policy, **I now take my hat off to them for this far-sighted act.** I add that in 1952, I myself benefitted from the scheme, and that is why I can sit back, retired, in some comfort in a middle-class suburb, and have croissants for breakfast when I want them.

Anyway, that is the end of my self-indulgence. Looking ahead, I happen to know that the dreadful war in Korea was halted in 1953, but the land was divided at the 38th Parallel into North and South, and that perpetuated the huge division of **what was previously one nation**. Then, on the economic front, no one would really expect **Australia** to recuperate over the course of next year, and so Fadden's words were just so much hot air.

Thoughts for the future. There was no doubt that the housing shortages would persist, that the roads outside our cities would continue to be disaster zones, and that our various pensioners would keep doing it impossibly hard. On the other hand, new family formation would continue at a merry rate, new houses would somehow be built, new cars and lawn mowers would be bought, and new children would grow up not even knowing that they were still suffering the hangover from the greatest war the world had ever seen.

But given all that in the mix, **1952 was a pretty good year.** It certainly beat the years ten, twenty, thirty and forty years before it. So, if you were born in 1952, and taking the good with the bad, I suggest you relax and content yourself with the idea **that things might have been better, but they surely could have been a lot worse.**

COMMENTS FROM READERS

Tom Lynch, Spears Point…..Some history writers make the mistake of trying to boost their authority by including graphs and charts all over the place. You on the other hand get a much better effect by saying things like "he made a pile". Or "every one worked hours longer that they should have, and felt like death warmed up at the end of the shift." I have seen other writers waste two pages of statistics painting the same picture as you did in a few words….

Barry Marr, Adelaide….you know that I am being facetious when I say that I wish the war had gone on for years longer so that you would have written more books about it…

Edna College, Auburn…. A few times I stopped and sobbed as you brought memories of the postman delivering letters, and the dread that ordinary people felt as he neared. How you captured those feelings yet kept your coverage from becoming maudlin or bogged down is a wonder to me….

Betty Kelly. Every time you seem to be getting serious you throw in a phrase or memory that lightens up the mood. In particular, in the war when you were describing the terrible carnage of Russian troops, you ended with a ten line description of how aggrieved you felt and ended it with "apart from that, things are pretty good here". For me, it turned the unbearable into the bearable, and I went from feeling morbid and angry back to a normal human being….

Alan Davey, Brisbane….I particularly liked the light-hearted way you described the scenes at the airports as the American high-flying entertainers flew in. I had always seen the crowd behaviour as disgraceful, but your light-hearted description of it made me realise it was in fact harmless and just good fun….

MORE INFORMATION ON THESE BOOKS

Over the past 16 years the author, Ron Williams, has written this series of books that present a social history of Australia in the post-war period. They cover the period for 1939 to 1968, with one book for each year. Thus there are 30 books.

To capture the material for each book, the author, Ron Williams, worked his way through the Sydney Morning Herald and the Age/Argus day-by-day, and picked out the best stories, ideas and trivia. He then wrote them up into 176 pages of a year-book.

He writes in a direct conversational style, he has avoided statistics and charts, and has produced easily-read material that is entertaining, and instructive, and charming.

They are invaluable as gifts for birthdays, Christmas, and anniversaries, and for the oldies who are hard to buy for.

These books are available at all major retailers. They are listed also in all leading catalogues, including Title Page and Dymocks and Booktopia.

Over the nexr few pages, summaries of other books years from 1939 to 1972 in the Series are presented. A synopsis of all books in the Series is available at:

www.boombooks.biz

THERE ARE 34 TITLES IN THIS SERIES
For the 34 years from 1939 to 1972

In 1954, Queen Elizabeth II was sent here victorious, and Petrov was our very own spy - what a thrill. Boys were being sentenced to life. Johnny Ray cried all the way to the bank. Church halls were being used for dirty dancing. Open the pubs after six? Were they ever shut? A-bombs had scaredies scared.

In 1955, be careful of the demon drink, get your brand new Salk injections, submit your design for the Sydney Opera house now, prime your gelignite for another Redex Trial, and stop your greyhounds killing cats. Princess Margaret shocked the Church, Huxley shocked the Bishops, and our Sundays are far from shocking.

****

Chrissi and birthday books for Mum and Dad and Aunt and Uncle and cousins and family and friends and work and everyone else.

Don't forget a good read and chuckle for yourself.

In 1956, the first big issue was the Suez crisis, which put our own Bob Menzies on the world stage, but he got no applause. TV was turned on in time for the Melbourne Olympics, Hungary was invaded and the Iron Curtain got a lot thicker. There was much concern about cruelty to sharks, and the horrors of country pubs persisted.

In 1957, Britain's Red Dean said Chinese Reds were OK. America avoided balance-of-payments problems by sending entertainers here. Sydney's Opera House will use lotteries to raise funds. The Russians launched Sputnik and a dog got a free ride. A bodkin crisis shook the nation.

****

These books, soft cover and hard cover, are available from the one-stop shop at:

www.boombooks.biz

In 1958, the Christian Brothers bought a pub and raffled it. Circuses were losing animals at a great rate. Officials were in hot water because the Queen Mother wasn't given a sun shade; it didn't worry the lined-up school children, they just fainted as normal. School milk was hot news, bread home deliveries were under fire. The RSPCA was killing dogs in a gas chamber.

****

HARD COVERS FOR 1939, 1949, 1959, 1969

AND 1940, 1950, 1960, 1970

SOFT COVER FOR ALL YEARS FROM 1939 TO 1972

EXPRESS POST AVAILABLE

www.boomooks.biz